WE CAN'T BREATHE

Dec 18

ALSO BY JABARI ASIM

NONFICTION

Not Guilty: Twelve Black Men Speak Out on the Law,
Justice, and Life (editor)

The N Word: Who Can Say It, Who Shouldn't, and Why

What Obama Means: For Our Politics, Our Country, Our Future

FICTION

A Taste of Honey: Stories

Only the Strong: An American Novel

CHILDREN'S

The Road to Freedom

Whose Toes Are Those?

Whose Knees Are These?

Daddy Goes to Work

Girl of Mine

Boy of Mine

Fifty Cents and a Dream

Preaching to the Chickens

A Child's Introduction to African American History

WE CAN'T BREATHE

ON BLACK LIVES, WHITE LIES, AND THE ART OF SURVIVAL

Jabari Asim

PICADOR

New York

picadorusa.com • instagram.com/picador
twitter.com/picadorusa • facebook.com/picadorusa

Picador® is a U.S. registered trademark and is used by Macmillan Publishing Group, LLC, under license from Pan Books Limited.

For book club information, please visit facebook.com/picadorbookclub or email marketing@picadorusa.com.

Two of these essays appeared in slightly different form in *Solstice* and *The Crisis* magazines.

The author would like to thank the John Simon Guggenheim Foundation for its generous support.

Designed by Steven Seighman

Library of Congress Cataloging-in-Publication Data

Names: Asim, Jabari, 1962– author.
Title: We can't breathe : on black lives, white lies, and the art of survival / Jabari Asim.
Other titles: We cannot breathe
Description: First Edition. | New York : Picador, [2018] | Includes bibliographical references.
Identifiers: LCCN 2018022983 | ISBN 9781250174536 (trade pbk.) | ISBN 9781250174512 (ebook)
Subjects: LCSH: African Americans—Social conditions. | African Americans—History. | Racism—United States—History. | United States—Race relations | Restorative justice—United States.
Classification: LCC E185 .A86 2018 | DDC 305.896/073—dc23
LC record available at https://lccn.loc.gov/2018022983

Our books may be purchased in bulk for promotional, educational, or business use. Please contact your local bookseller or the Macmillan Corporate and Premium Sales Department at 1-800-221-7945, extension 5442, or by email at MacmillanSpecialMarkets@macmillan.com.

First Edition: October 2018

10 9 8 7 6 5 4 3 2 1

For Liana, for always

CONTENTS

Your silence will not protect you.
> —Audre Lorde, "The Transformation of
> Silence into Language and Action"

Who will speak these days,
if not I,
if not you?
—Muriel Rukeyser, "The Speed of Darkness"

WE CAN'T BREATHE

GETTING IT TWISTED

In my childhood home, we were not allowed to call each other liars. It fueled my father's indignation. Slung with the casual malice that only bickering siblings can summon, *Liar!* somehow set off a warning beacon, alerting my father wherever he was. A schoolteacher with a reputation for discipline, he wasn't remotely as stern as my friends imagined. But proper speech was an area he patrolled with diligence, and his radar was remarkably sensitive. Lazy enunciation, insults, and vulgarities were the blunders most likely to set him off. Once, in the middle of an argument, I told my brother to drop dead. My father's admonishment was calmly but pointedly delivered, and even now my ears burn at the memory of it. His catalogue of deplorable lingo was expansive and, to our considerable confusion, unpredictable. Words that hardly raised other parents' eyebrows could quickly draw his ire, words like *butt*, *funk*, and especially—inexplicably—*liar*.

No such codes existed beyond our front yard, and the streets presented delectable opportunities to mix it up with the neighborhood kids. We gave as well as we got, diving into the exchange of insults and threats like stragglers in the desert plunging into a sparkling oasis. If we caught someone making an assertion without evidence to back it up, we unleashed our vernacular and let the culprit have it. The local dialect turned *you're a liar* into *you a lie*, a contraction I found irresistible despite my father's prohibitions. I appreciated the way it transformed a person into the very thing they were accused of.

Our lies and tall tales usually revolved around girls or athletic exploits and were only occasionally malicious. They were lighthearted fabrications inspired and shaped by the stories we heard at the feet of our fathers, in barbershops and on front porches, at barbecues and ball games. For black people in the 1960s, even less welcomed as full-fledged members of society than we are today, yarn-spinning presented a rare American ritual in which we could freely participate. Other venerable traditions, like burning our neighbors alive, casting a ballot, or taking communion alongside white Christians, had long been denied us. But lying, now that was an equal-opportunity activity. With roots in stories about Aunt Nancy, Brer Rabbit, and John Henry, our inventions were small-scale variations on the African American experience, more about outwitting the powerful than manipulating privilege at the expense of the weak. Our bluster was closer in style to Troy Maxson recalling his tussles with Death in *Fences* than, say, Thomas Jefferson arguing in *Notes on the State of Virginia* that orangutans find black women sexy. Those differences aside, what could be more American than pretending truths were self-evident when they seldom were? What could be more American than dressing up a lie in tailor-made language, like romanticizing treason as a Lost Cause or sugarcoating genocide by rebranding it as Manifest Destiny? As a bulwark against the realities of life in a racist republic, our fictions helped us believe we belonged.

In our world, the consequences of being caught in a lie were usually no harsher than school-yard ridicule or parental discipline. A person could get grounded or "put on punishment," as neighborhood parlance would have it. Our falsehoods possessed little power to influence another person's circumstances or alter a destiny, and we understood that their relative impotence stemmed more from our blackness than our youth. Anyone could see that "I blamed that broken window on Johnny and he got put on punishment" was a far cry from "I accused that nigger boy of whistling at me and he got strangled, chopped up, and tossed in the river."

Recently, listening to a white man's story on NPR got me thinking again about untruths and consequences. At age ninety-four, Joseph Linsk disclosed a lie he'd enabled when he was eight years old. He stole two dollars to pay off a debt and said nothing when his mother blamed the theft on Pearl, the family's black cleaning lady. She lost her job and was unable to get another because of her tainted reputation. Linsk remained silent and grew up to become a prosperous physician. Years later, he called on NPR listeners to help him locate Pearl's family so that he could try to make amends. Carrying the burden of guilt for so long, he admitted, had left him "smitten with grief." Such a lovely, complicated phrase. Smitten as in struck down, or as in enamored with? And if Linsk considered himself unbearably tormented, one wonders how he would have assessed Pearl's feelings. I'm tempted to conclude that Linsk, like too many white Americans, was less concerned with restorative justice than with assuaging his own pain.

When I posted a link to his story on Facebook, friends' responses eloquently lamented the long tradition of white lies leading to disastrous outcomes for black people. Yet my favorite comment was the most succinct: "Hmph!" That single syllable epitomized the tangled web encompassing whites' misdeeds and the desire for absolution from the people they've wronged. The ritual is often seen with representatives from the media thrusting their microphones at traumatized African Americans while their wounds are still gushing blood. Effectively serving as proxies for the white gaze, the reporters demand to know if the unlucky sufferers are ready to forgive their assailants, usually police officers or armed vigilantes tragically warped by delusions of supremacy (see Zimmerman, George). On the periphery, public officials hover uncertainly, trembling like Jefferson considering the prospect of a just God. To take the pressure off themselves, appointees and officeholders place it firmly on their bereaved black constituents by suggesting that healing cannot commence until they indicate their willingness to put the transgression behind them. It would be even more helpful if they could also express faith that justice will be done in court or, failing that, heaven. A forgiving victim who remembers to discourage street protests before pausing to pray for the killer will do more to "restore trust" than any indictment or conviction ever could. Reviewing footage of several of these predictable ceremonies made me think of an essay I'd read by the British writer Hilary Mantel. "Oppressors don't just want to do their deed," she wrote, "they want to take a bow: they want their victims to sing their praises."

The history of our Revolution will be one continued lie from one end to the other. —JOHN ADAMS

Along with brutality, torture, and murder, a principal step in oppression, American style has long involved getting between the oppressed and their stories. Depending on the circumstances, intervention may involve disputing oppressed people's versions of events, distorting them or seizing them outright, or renaming and repurposing them. Nurturing the lie at the heart of each method, a maneuver known in some locales as "getting it twisted," helps oppressors sustain what Toni Morrison calls the "master narrative." When individuals in some African American communities get things twisted, often beginning their tale with *What happened was*, a popular response is *Who I look like? Boo Boo the fool?* The question is quickly recognized as a way of announcing one's refusal to be bamboozled, hoodwinked, or misled. But street-level skepticism is one thing; collective willingness to accept the lie of American exceptionalism is quite another. Many descendants of enslaved Africans are no less intentionally gullible than their countrymen in wanting the American tradition—and the white men who established it—to be uniformly virtuous. For example, we know that more than a century before Thomas Dixon and D. W. Griffith started writing lies with lightning, the Framers were dipping them in ink and inscribing them on parchment. Despite the dishonesty inherent in their secular scriptures, the disheartening fractions and lies of omission, we want the nation's founders to be flawless. We want to believe that one youthful misadventure with a cherry tree was all a typical Great White Father needed to set him on the right path. We want to believe that the original plutocrats were never vain or insecure, that they were never unfaithful lovers or abusive husbands, that they never kept black women in chains and raped them repeatedly, that they never suffered from tooth decay and body odor or knew the heartbreak of psoriasis and regrettable habits. In my old neighborhood this kind of naïveté was called falling for the okey-doke.

Benjamin Banneker, an early American genius, was

admirably resistant to willful amnesia. In 1791, he became aware of Jefferson's exuberant lies about black people in *Notes on the State of Virginia*. They included:

- Black people were more inclined toward lust than whites, but not sufficiently sophisticated to appreciate or experience the complexities of genuine romantic love.
- It was only natural for black men to prefer the superior beauty of white women, just as the orangutan "preferred black women over those of his own species."
- Pain, both emotional and physical, was "less felt and sooner forgotten" among blacks.
- Blacks were "induced by the slightest amusements," "had dull, tasteless and anomalous" imaginations, and were incapable of uttering "a thought above the level of plain narration."

Jefferson's whiteness was so fragile that a profligate lifestyle utterly dependent on human trafficking, sexual exploitation, and coerced labor was not enough. He had to buttress it with deliberate falsehoods designed to comfort the planter class and allay their fears of rebellious blackness. Incensed, Banneker called him on it. Including an edition of his almanac with a letter dated August 20, 1791, he wrote:

> *Sir, how pitiable is it to reflect, that although you were so fully convinced of the benevolence of the Father of Mankind, and of his equal and impartial distribution of these rights and privileges, which he hath conferred upon them, that you should at the same time counteract his*

*mercies, in detaining by fraud and violence so numer-
ous a part of my brethren, under groaning captivity and
cruel oppression, that you should at the same time be
found guilty of that most criminal act, which you pro-
fessedly detested in others, with respect to yourselves.*

In other words, Sir, you a lie.

Jefferson's letter in reply was tepid and noncommittal:

Sir,

*I thank you, sincerely, for your letter of the 19th instant,
and for the Almanac it contained. No body wishes more
than I do, to see such proofs as you exhibit, that nature
has given to our black brethren talents equal to those of
the other colors of men; and that the appearance of the
want of them, is owing merely to the degraded condition
of their existence, both in Africa and America. I can
add with truth, that no body wishes more ardently to see
a good system commenced, for raising the condition,
both of their body and mind, to what it ought to be, as
far as the imbecility of their present existence, and other
circumstances, which cannot be neglected, will admit.*

*I have taken the liberty of sending your Almanac to
Monsieur de Condozett, Secretary of the Academy of
Sciences at Paris, and Member of the Philanthropic Society, because I considered it as a document, to which
your whole color had a right for their justification,
against the doubts which have been entertained of them.*

*I am with great esteem, Sir, Your most obedient
Humble Servant,*

Thomas Jefferson.

He made no attempt to directly address or refute any of Banneker's objections, sidestepping such provocations as *fraud*, *violence*, and *cruel* while tossing back an *imbecility* of his own. That kind of verbal thrust-and-parry, with its sly implications, coy dismissals, and passive-aggressive misdirection continues to shape disputes between whites and Americans of color over the nature of reality, a conflict I like to describe as narrative combat. Years later, Jefferson speculated in a letter to a friend that Banneker probably had (white) assistance in performing the calculations for the almanac and had possessed a mind "of very common stature indeed." In the end he let the lies stand.

Jefferson was not an elected official when he presented his inflammatory and patently false "observations" of black people to the world. Although he was minister to France the year he published his *Notes*, he was opining as a private citizen. Yet he was a public figure of considerable stature and thus his influence can't be overestimated. His notes enlivened stereotypes that resonate even today. When a white mother called the police in Washington, DC, because black teens near an ATM made her "uncomfortable"—and police unquestionably followed her implicit commands by detaining the youngsters—that was race-based lying at work. When the manager of a lingerie store made all the black customers leave after a black woman was caught shoplifting, that was race-based lying at work.

A different but no less caustic danger results from the liar acting as an agent of the state. When the state gets it twisted, as it did in the case of the Central Park Five, the consequences are long-ranging and irreparable. After a white woman was raped and beaten nearly to death in Central Park in 1989, the Manhattan district attorney's sex-crime unit railroaded five innocent young black and Latino men into prison. Each served between five and twelve years. The state's mendacity was abetted by the defendants' coerced confessions: vague, inconsistent statements in which they lied on themselves. Years later, after another man confessed to the crime and the Five were exonerated, former district attorney Linda Fairstein, who had supervised the sex-crime unit, continued to ignore the complete absence of evidence and insist that the jury had reached the correct verdict. Donald Trump, who had fanned the flames of derision by purchasing full-page ads in local newspapers calling for "muggers and murderers" to suffer for their crimes, also expressed no remorse. "They admitted they were guilty," he said in a statement to CNN. "The police doing the original investigation say they were guilty. The fact that that case was settled with so much evidence against them is outrageous." There was no evidence against them, and investigators found no DNA from any of the young men at the scene of the crime. Like Jefferson and many others before them, Fairstein and Trump refused to admit their roles in perpetuating a toxic deception, even when facts inconveniently illuminated their errors.

> *Deceiving Americans is one of the few growing home industries we still have in this country.*
> —CHARLES SIMIC, "AGE OF IGNORANCE"

In 1988, Newt Gingrich spoke passionately of a war against liberals that had to be "fought with a scale and a duration and a savagery that is only true of civil wars," a war in which language would be wielded as "a key mechanism of control." Two years later his political organization, GOPAC, offered aspiring Republican candidates a key list of words and phrases—*sick, pathetic, radical,* and *welfare*, among them—to help voters distinguish between them and their Democratic opponents. If not for such maneuvers, it would be tempting to identify something unprecedented in Trump's aggressive pseudo-populist postures during the campaign, as well as his tendency to dismiss any coverage that challenges his narrative as merely *fake news*. Instead, his tactics remind us that getting it twisted is hardly a new method for the GOP. It is the party of Atwater, after all, and the party whose most popular president in recent decades launched his campaign in Philadelphia, Mississippi, where the bodies of three activists were found during the height of the civil rights battle in that state. Perhaps because of that sordid history, it was just a short spiral from Ronald Reagan's welfare queens to Trump's wilding teens, Mexican rapists, death panels, and gay Kenyan Muslims masquerading as American presidents. Our Twitter-happy narcissist in chief, continuing his long history of dissembling and prevarication, rode into power on a wave of such shouts and murmurs (and dog whistles). The "mainstream" press, suffering from an embarrassing lack of diversity, did little to resist Trump's verbal tsunami, using *working class* as a euphemism for white people, often uncritically accepting police accounts of shootings involving unarmed black people, and showing a woeful reluctance to identify racists as the unprincipled degenerates they are. The day after Trump declared his candidacy, Dylann Roof executed nine black Charleston churchgoers. As black communities nationwide reeled in horror, initial news reports described the unrepentant assassin as "a bug-eyed boy with a bowl haircut who came from a broken home," a waif so bedraggled and forlorn that local cops took him for sandwiches before hauling him to jail. Similarly, the media, preoccupied with the prep-school costumes favored by Trump's youthful troops, failed to seriously consider the visceral trauma resulting from resurgent racist terror. A month before the election, *Mother Jones* magazine introduced Richard Spencer as if he were a new neighbor at the block-party cookout. "Meet the dapper white nationalist riding the Trump wave," its promoting tweet cooed. Similarly, ten days after Trump's victory, the *Los Angeles Times* encouraged readers to "Meet the new think tank in town: the 'alt-right' comes to Washington." The dithering over the appropriateness of using *alt-right*, *white nationalist*, etc. was a sideshow that helped us to avoid the fundamental questions that must be confronted: Is voting for a racist itself a racist act? Can one commit a racist act and not be a racist? Until we delve into that riddle, no real conversation can take place between those who voted for the forty-fifth president and those who did not.

Similarly, I find little purpose in referring to the Richard Spencers and Donald Trumps of this world as advocates of "white supremacy." To use that term, even while condemning it, is to flirt recklessly with absurdity, and uttering it even in that context leaves a rancid, intolerable taste. I'd like to suggest that it has outlived its usefulness. As a phrase describing a specific psychosis deriving from a race-based lie, *white insanity* seems far more suitable.

And while we're at it, self-styled liberals might consider arming their own vocabularies. Help those Americans who support full equality for all human beings by using words like the following to describe those who oppose it:

Duplicitous	Divisive
Greedy	Unethical
Racist	Intellectually challenged

Delusional	Confederate
Psychotic	Covetous
Selfish	Sadistic
Paranoid	Cunning
Ammosexual	Uppity
Sterile	Confused
Flaccid	Malignant

It's time to replace the timid discourse of pragmatic centrism with the aggressive language our situation requires. Unlike Barack Obama, who spent both terms of his presidency hamstrung by conventional notions of propriety and understandably wary of coming off as an "angry black man," the rest of us have license to speak freely—and speak out. "It is a very grave question as to whether or not the slavery and degradation of Negroes in America has not been unnecessarily prolonged by the submission to evil," W. E. B. DuBois once observed. Replace the archaic-sounding *evil* with *blatant corruption* and the question applies not just to black people but also to any American who's not a member of the gilded one percent. As I watch the forty-fifth president and his lackeys attack the tender flesh of opponents, with claws fully extended and fangs dripping saliva, I can't help thinking of Benjamin Franklin's words to his sister Jane. "If you make yourself a Sheep," he wrote, "the Wolves will eat you."

> *. . . this whole country is full of lies*
> *You're all gonna die and die like flies*
> —NINA SIMONE, "MISSISSIPPI GODDAM"

Lately, I've been revisiting the work of Ronald Fair, an inexcusably unsung writer. I admire him not only because his deeply empathetic portraits of black boys and men encourage my own literary ambitions. I also admire him because he laid out the structure of narrative combat as well as any American novelist ever has. Especially in his books *Hog Butcher* (1966) and *We Can't Breathe* (1972), Fair exposed the limitations inherent in what he called "this lie they call democracy, this insidious myth they call fair play, this vicious thing called the-American-way-of-life."

Both novels address issues that continue to resonate today, including economic inequality, a legal system designed to promote white impunity and accumulate black convictions, and the ferocity with which whiteness challenges black people's right to narrate their own experiences.

Like Richard Wright and Gwendolyn Brooks, Fair took readers inside the tenements and kitchenettes of South Side Chicago. Like August Wilson, he created characters who insist on reevaluating the wisdom of the Great Migration. What is the point of them fleeing north, they ask, if they are only going to encounter the very conditions they fled? Fair called the myths of a liberal North "glorious fantasies about a new and better world," but refugees from Dixie turned a deaf ear to skeptics. Huddled masses of black people, yearning to breathe free, broke for St. Louis, Chicago, Harlem, and Detroit like displaced European tribes hell-bent for Ellis Island. But when they arrived, they sometimes discovered there wasn't enough air to go around.

"We came to the North, and we're still victims of discrimination and oppression in the North," Wilson complained in an interview. "The real reason that the people left was a search for jobs, because the agriculture, cotton agriculture in particular, could no longer support us. But the move to the cities has not been a good move. Today . . . we still don't have jobs. The last time blacks in America were working was during the Second World War, when there was a need for labor, and it did not matter what color you were."

Whereas Wilson saw the Great Migration as a mistake, Ernie Johnson, the observant young man at the center of *We Can't Breathe*, sees the epic journey as the result of a lie of omission. "I read about the South and things whites had done to my people there," he says, "and I wondered why more people had not written about atrocities in the North—in many ways they were worse because they were committed behind a smiling face that always kept you thinking that things were going to be better."

Ernie's neighborhood differs little from that of Wilford Robinson, the headstrong young hero of *Hog Butcher*. The landmarks, hurdles, and pitfalls of their 1960s-era Chicago streets would not be out of place in Tamir Rice's Cleveland or Trayvon Martin's Sanford, Florida. Ernie, developing the sharp eye of the novelist he hopes to become, has already recognized the local policemen as "assassins for white society." Similarly, Wilford sees the motorcycle cops who menace his community as "a special squad created not so much to protect them as to keep them in line." The plots of both books hinge on the protagonist witnessing a police killing of an unarmed black man. With social media and cell phones still a twinkle in a technologist's eye, all each boy has is his own account versus the official story that the police will tell.

When Ernie tells his father what he has seen, they discuss going to the state's attorney. Ernie deduces a world of significance from his parents' exchange of glances. "He looked at my mother and I could see how desperately he was trying to find the right thing to say, how he was trying to save himself in my eyes as a man, how he was trying to give me something meaningful to hang on to for the rest of my life, a feeling of fairness about our world if nothing else."

His father concludes that going to the state's attorney would be a misstep that could end disastrously. The solution, he says, is to take control of the narrative. "Write it down," he advises Ernie, who is about to enter high school. "Write down how much a black man has to pay for bein' a black man in this country. Write down what happened here today so the whole damn world'll know what we take just to do the simple things we do, and let them see if they'd be strong enough to be black." With no hope of justice for the slain black man, Ernie and his family dream of redemption in the form of the art he will someday create.

In *Hog Butcher*, a precinct captain stops by Wilford's house to intimidate him into silence before he can testify about what he has seen. "It's not that we don't want you to tell the truth," he says to the boy. "It's just that we don't want you to say anything just now. Now that's not tellin' a lie, is it?"

But Wilford remembers his teacher's advice: "If you know somebody else is tellin' a story and you don't say nothin' about it, well, then, that's the same as you tellin' a story right with 'em." Unlike our nonagenarian friend in the NPR segment, Wilford realizes that enabling a lie will leave him entangled in remorse.

Wilford's experience appears headed to a hopeful resolution when his steadfast bravery moves a black policeman to breach the thin blue line of silence. On the witness stand, the cop resolves to free himself from a timeless trap pitting "black man against black man to maintain a goddamn white lie."

Ernie, the author's alter ego, continues to face bitter circumstances but regards them with a defiant glare. "I was extremely cold, but my mind was occupied with a story that I wanted to write about the North," he confides, "a story that I felt no one would believe or take seriously. Undoubtedly, it was something that had happened to someone's cousin or uncle or brother or father, and was told over the years from black neighborhood to neighborhood, from city to city, north and south, until I finally heard it. I don't remember having been told the whole story, only certain aspects of it. I knew it would be good, and I also knew that the truth of this story would be denied by whites. But I was going to write it anyway." Nearly a half century before it became a battle cry prompted by the police killing of Eric Garner, Ronald Fair made *We Can't Breathe* a ringing declaration of intent.

Echoing his resolve, we continue to write—and resist. In the tradition of black bards known and unknown, we compose with purposeful fury. We muster our candor and eloquence against a master narrative advising us to patiently attend those who continue to cling so eagerly to antiblack racism, to sit with folded hands and hear them out. It's what we might call a morality tale, a parable in which embracing white people at their worst inspires them to return the gesture and open their arms to us in all our complicated, flawed, and wonderful coloredness. The warmth of our newfound mutual affection will be so intense and contagious that it softens hardened minds and changes the direction of the American future. It's a story that requires a substantial suspension of disbelief.

Or it's simply another lie.

We walk in outer space, but we can't walk the streets of Cicero.

— Martin Luther King Jr.

THE ELEMENTS OF STRUT

In ideal circumstances, the human body flows in a state of strut. A jauntiness, an ease. A response to the rhythms that animate the earth. To strut is to reflect the graceful rotation of the planet in one's breath, in one's step, in the pace and melody of one's speech, in one's swerve and laughter. I strut, therefore I am.

Strut is the body in motion, occupying, manipulating, and moving through space. Strutting requires freedom, the liberty to flex and stretch. Lately, I have been habitually watching a short film by Andrew Margetson. His camera follows the brilliant dancer Lil Buck as he floats, pops, and glides through the Fondation Louis Vuitton in Paris. Dancers are often so supple they can't help themselves, walking with a distinctive grace that signals their talent. Lil Buck doesn't walk like that. He enters the museum as any ordinary mortal would. He is lithe and trim, to be sure, but with an unassuming gait that hides his kinetic genius. Then the music begins and he leans into the air, his ankles as improbably bent as a hapless guard defending LeBron James. His voice-over narration introduces his style as a blend of hip-hop and ballet. "As performing artists, as dancers," he explains, "we see everything as art." Up the escalator and through a light-filled space adorned with paintings, Lil Buck maneuvers his undeniably dark body, pirouetting, altering time and gently challenging gravity. He bends to the point of crumpling, only to reassemble, restoring his smooth musculature as if by magic.

The beauty of the dance is a timely distraction. Lil Buck moves adroitly in a space where figures like his have seldom been regarded with respect or delight. His sublime whirl helps me forget, however briefly, that darkness in a body complicates even the most basic stroll, reduces an inalienable right to an elusive privilege.

The unbound black body is profoundly inconvenient. The dark muscles, the bones underneath, the vulnerable organs, and the sheltering skin—each comprises a segment on the map of a plundered continent, each is redolent of conquest and empire. Four centuries ago, our ancestors were marched at gunpoint across sand and savannah, far from their home villages to near-death and misery in the confinement castles of the African west coast. Those who stumbled and lost their footing never made it even that far. Inevitably, history complicates our strut.

Then as now, locomotion sometimes can require treading the slender border between life and death. Lately, headlines remind us of all the same and different ways a black body can collide with its inconvenience. Breathing. Walking. Waiting to cross at the light. Using a golf club as a cane while crossing a Seattle intersection. Heading home while carrying candy and a can of ice tea. Any of these can be seen as unforgivable trespass, alien intrusion on ground that must be defended. The wrongful arrests; the point-blank executions; the gunshots to the back; the militarized police responses; the illuminating silence of white self-styled liberals and, most critical, the paucity of convictions all point to the same existential question: How can we strut in a strange land?

Have I thought of the body as sanctuary?
—LIA PURPURA, "ON LOOKING"

While my contemplation of strut respects the question of how to live in a black body, I am more interested in how to escape my own imprisoning concept of that body. I don't believe the black body has any more potential than any other kind, but I am concerned with the extent to which its capabilities are suppressed by one's own internalized limitations. Racism and its accompanying cruelties have shaped me to police myself, to restrict my own movement through spaces. And by spaces I mean both actual and metaphorical. The great Resister Carter G. Woodson warned, "If you can control a man's thinking you do not have to worry about his action." He might have added, *Independent thinking seldom goes undisciplined.* Some black people use this fact to justify subjecting their children to corporal punishment. They contend, incorrectly, "I beat my son so the police won't." On any given day, how often do I manage to keep oppressive thinking out of my head? Am I ever free from an imagined white gaze? How often do I succumb to beating myself?

If he should Runaway, he must wear a Pothook about his neck, and if that won't bring him under, he must wear Iron spaneals upon his Legs till you are pretty sure he will be orderly; for as he is my slave he must and shall be obedient, but if he be orderly use him kindly. —JOSEPH BALL, COLONIAL PLANTER

When my wife and I visited the National Museum of African American History and Culture during its opening weekend, immense crowds made it impossible to linger before any of the exhibits. Still, it was easy to make connections between past and present even while moving rapidly. Easy, for example, to note the painful irony of tolerating forced, elbow-to-elbow intimacy with strangers in underground passageways while looking at displays about the cramped horrors of the Middle Passage. Easy to look at shackles and think of Alton Sterling, executed by police a few months earlier while bound and subdued in Baton Rouge, or Kajieme Powell: after killing the mentally disturbed man, St. Louis police officers rolled his corpse over and cuffed his inert wrists behind his lifeless back, as if mocking that whole freedom-in-death thing. Similarly, it was hard to look at images of Africans chained in the holds of storm-tossed trading vessels and not think of Freddie Gray, shackled in the back of a speeding Baltimore police van, on a rough ride to his death. Hard to avoid the unsightly realization that rusted iron manacles from the mid-1800s, forged specifically to hold a black body in place, still look sturdy enough to do the job.

I could find little information on the "spaneals" Joseph Ball referred to in his letter. He may have been referring to an iron version of *spancels*, which, according to the dictionary, are noosed ropes used "to hobble an animal, especially a horse or cow." Owner of the Epping Forest plantation in colonial Virginia, Ball enslaved and traded human beings from Africa until his death in the early eighteenth century. His nephew, George Washington, was also obsessed with policing the mobility of his enslaved. In Henry Wiencek's book *An Imperfect God*, the historian writes that the man who would become president "created a new problem he called 'night walking'—men and women going out at night to visit family members. A man named Boson, who was twice caught running away in 1760, may actually have been night walking to visit his lover when he was caught." Yet, do I marvel at the complexity of such a strut, the strategy and fortitude employed in traveling great distances, avoiding paddy rollers under cover of darkness, indulging hurried kisses and urgent embraces before rushing back to begin the day's drudgery.

Ball and Washington were long dead by 1849, when Supreme Court chief justice Roger B. Taney weighed in on the intricacies of strut. In his dissent in the *Passenger Cases*, he wrote, "We are all citizens of the United States; and as members of the same community, must have the right to pass and repass through every part of it without interruption, as freely as in our own States." The court's decision in *Passenger* struck down laws in New York and Massachusetts involving the collection of head taxes on incoming immigrants. But, as Kunal M. Parker points out in *The Cambridge History of Law in America*, "Beneath this constitutional debate lay the explosive question of whether free blacks were part of the community of U.S. citizens and, as such, whether they possessed the right to travel throughout national territory." Eight years later, in *Dred Scott v. Sandford*, Chief Justice Taney would explain exactly whom he meant by "we." He declared that black people "had no rights which the white man was bound to respect," casting Scott's desire to strut to free territory as an affront that the South would consider grounds for war.

Their debasement reaffirmed by Taney's court, both the enslaved and those tethered by subtler bonds continued to rely on culture for solace and even transcendence, however brief. In jubas, ring shouts, and cakewalks, black bodies turned and pranced with rhythm, delicacy, and commitment, as if they could strut all the way to Africa or, failing that, a territory where slavery had been banned. As they stepped and whirled through war and its aftermath, as the contours of their collective strut distorted and bent under the ignorant gaze of their captors, as movements that began as parody became subjects of parody themselves (blackface minstrelsy), their motions must have acquired a melancholy knowingness. Yet, they pressed on, dipping, wheeling, and risking delight.

With the Southern Rebellion ostensibly resolved in their favor, the newly "emancipated" were no doubt inclined to waltz directly from the fields and quarters to the beckoning world, the postbellum precursor to dancing in the streets. But in their initial jubilation they struggled to withstand a new reality in which they stood unshackled but remained unfree. That condition was already familiar to those who had earlier slipped through the cracks the Rebellion had created. Desperate and with few friends or resources, they followed the conquering footsteps of the Union Army. "Neither soldier nor fugitive speaks with so deep a meaning as that dark human cloud that clung like remorse on the rear of those swift columns, swelling at times to half their size, almost engulfing and choking them," DuBois wrote in *The Souls of Black Folk*. "In vain were they ordered back, in vain were bridges hewn from beneath their feet; on they trudged and writhed and surged, until they rolled into Savannah, a starved and naked horde of tens of thousands." Blackness to a ragged thinness beat shines nonetheless: in the midst of filth and misery, the refugees shared sustenance and intelligence, forming new alliances of bond and blood. They made a way out of no way, just as their ancestors had done in the sweltering bellies of *Jesus*, *Amistad*, *Henrietta Marie*, and the other vessels that had dragged them, battered and tormented, to the looming horrors of a strange new hell.

Sometimes, I picture in my mind a crimson thread originating in Africa, unspooling alongside a young boy stumbling and choking as his coffle yanks him toward the sea. The thread extends apparently without end, through the bloody spill of centuries and across fruited plains and fetid plantations, trailing the double-time stomp of a black Union soldier and continuing to unspool beside the swollen ankles of a church matron marching her way from Selma to Montgomery. I could see the thread snaking along Pennsylvania Avenue during Barack and Michelle Obama's stately walk to the White House. It's a spirit-lifting fantasy of black endurance and triumph, a useful antidote for the Weary Blues. I imagine the black refugees that DuBois wrote about might have been similarly revived by the sight of dark-skinned soldiers garbed in Union blue, counting off cadences while picking them up and putting them down. Just such a scene unfolds in *Glory*, the Oscar-winning 1989 film about the mostly black 54th Massachusetts Volunteer Infantry. A group of black children scurry across a yard and line up at a picket fence to gape and grin at the regiment as they proceed down a Southern lane, rifles poised on their shoulders. With fifes and drums providing accompaniment, Morgan Freeman, portraying Sgt. Maj. John Rawlins, pauses to smile kindly at the children. "That's right," he tells them. "Ain't no dream. We run away slaves but we come back fighting men." The children, bathed in a sepia glow, stare in awe at the soldiers' retreating ranks. In the background, a choir sings soaring angelic notes.

By the end of the Rebellion, nearly 200,000 black men

had helped defend the Republic against the Confederate traitors (179,000 in the Union Army, 19,000 in the Navy). At the same time, black women like Harriet Tubman engaged in a stealthier strut, risking their lives to assist the war effort by gathering intelligence behind enemy lines. While their deeds were inspiring to their fellow black people, most whites had quite a different reaction. For them, the notion of armed, marching Negroes was the stomach-churning stuff of nightmares, frequently involving the violation of white women and the pillaging of land claimed by whites. Instead of DuBois's starved and naked horde, they saw a weaponized and rapacious swarm, lockstep in bodacious strut. Marching—unarmed—would indeed become a favorite method for nonviolently protesting white "supremacy," especially as black activists and their allies came to rely increasingly on civil disobedience in the century to come. In the meantime, whites set about repairing their broken commonwealth. After a brief flirtation with genuine reform, they rushed to reconcile with their former enemies, easily finding common ground in a seductive compulsion to confine the black body to its proper place—geographical, social, and metaphorical. The black strut developed a dispiriting pattern: two steps forward, one step back.

> *There's a certain*
> *amount of traveling*
> *in a dream deferred.*
> —LANGSTON HUGHES, "SAME IN BLUES"

After the Hayes-Tilden compromise killed Reconstruction in 1877, the white American obsession with breaking people and things found release in the form of ritualized murders that involved torture, mutilation, burning, and communal immersion in a ceremony of sexual and religious fervor. Lynchings, as they came to be known, were a national pastime, like county fairs, Sunday school, and spectator sports. They continued in their principal form well into the 1950s, with occasional outbreaks occurring even now. The Equal Justice Initiative's recent comprehensive study found evidence of 4,075 lynchings of African Americans in the South between 1877 and 1950. That figure doesn't include the murders of Emmett Till in 1955 and James Byrd Jr. in 1998, to say nothing of the numberless killings that took place above the Mason-Dixon line during the same period. Perversely democratic, these blood rites claimed a variety of sacrificial victims, including children, expectant mothers, and fetuses ripped from wombs and nailed to trees. Not surprisingly, soldiers in uniform, whose sheer effrontery provoked such irrational horror, were often favorite targets.

While many lynchings focused on one or a small number of victims, the compulsion occasionally erupted with such orgiastic excess that it engulfed entire communities. The East St. Louis massacre of 1917 provides an appalling example. The factory town on the border between Illinois and Missouri had become contested ground after nearly twelve thousand blacks migrated there from the violent, unrepentant South. Conflicts between white workers and black newcomers blew up on July 2. A group of black people, fearing for their lives and standing their ground, returned fire at a car carrying two white men. The men were police officers, and both died instantly. Soon a mob of whites rampaged through the city, focusing their rage on "Black Valley," the African American community.

Carlos F. Hurd, a reporter with the *St. Louis Post-Dispatch*, published a chilling eyewitness account of small, leaderless groups, moving with "horribly cool deliberateness and a spirit of fun" as they set about "destroying the life of every discoverable black man." Their methods included stoning, bludgeoning, shooting, hanging, and burning victims alive. "The sheds in the rear of Negroes' houses, which were themselves in the rear of the main buildings on Fourth Street, had been ignited to drive out the Negro occupants of the houses," Hurd wrote. "And the slayers were waiting for them to come out. It was stay in and be roasted, or come out and be slaughtered. A moment before I arrived, one Negro had taken the desperate chance of coming out, and the rattle of revolver shots, which I heard as I approached the corner, was followed by the cry, 'They've got him!'"

Official reports listed thirty-nine dead black people, but others put the number much higher. The *St. Louis Globe-Democrat*'s banner headline declared, "100 Negroes Shot, Burned, Clubbed to Death in E. St. Louis Race War." Six thousand black residents fled, rushing headlong over the two bridges stretching across the Mississippi River and into St. Louis.

Forty-eight hours after the slaughter, Ida B. Wells arrived at the scene via train and disembarked with a purposeful strut. As president of the Chicago-based Negro Fellowship League (which included criminal injustice and lynching among its concerns), she had raised funds for the trip and set out to investigate the atrocity firsthand. She would have been in her midfifties then, a renowned anti-lynching activist and seasoned warrior in the battle for justice. Because of her superhuman qualities, I've always thought there should be an action figure based on her. She had survived being violently tossed from a segregated Southern train, biting one of her assailants, and battling the railroad in court. She had narrowly escaped death at the hands of enraged whites who burned her Memphis newspaper office and printing press to the ground. I can see her on the platform in East St. Louis, a determined beauty in a fine dress, a string of pearls, and her signature upsweep hairstyle. She holds her head high, eyes missing no detail as she makes her way to the scenes of the crime. "No one molested me in my walk from the station to the City Hall, although I did not see a single colored person until I reached the City Hall building," she later reported. A few feet away, black bodies lay smoldering in the wreckage of the barbarity, in mounds of charred viscera and bones, half-sunk in the rubble of their ruined homes and businesses, and submerged in hastily dug mass graves.

Wells joined forces with a Red Cross volunteer, assisting refugees as they gathered whatever belongings they had left. They told her their stories while traveling back and forth to St. Louis in a truck with an armed soldier at each end. Along with Hurd's report in the *Post-Dispatch* and DuBois's twenty-four-page report in *The Crisis*, Wells's oral histories remain some of the most reliable documentation of the massacre. Working tirelessly (so much so that she forgot to eat or drink), she spent the night in a municipal lodging house on the Missouri side. The place was packed with hundreds of displaced individuals and families.

Every which way we turned there were women and children and men, dazed over the thing that had come to them and unable to tell what it was all about. Most of them had left clothes and homes behind, thankful to have saved their lives and those of their families. Some of them had not located relatives and did not know whether the mob or fire had taken them. They lined the streets or were standing out on the grassy banks of the lawns that surround the City Hall, or stood in groups discussing their experiences. Red Cross and charitable workers gave them food to eat, and the city the place to sleep in the city lodging house, and some of them had clothing which they were issuing to these people who had suddenly been robbed of everything except what they stood in.

Back in Chicago, Wells and her allies used her report to challenge the governor of Illinois to do something, anything on behalf of the murdered and exiled. "No one has any feeling of certainty that anything will be done, either to punish the rioters or to make the lives and property of Negroes more secure permanently," she wrote. Wells went on to press her case with the federal government. Her committee's letter to Congress read in part, "The riot was no sudden outburst of passion. It was a combination of a publicly declared determination on the part of white laborers to drive colored laborers from work or kill them. There was no provocation by acts of lawless blacks, no drunkenness on the part of the whites—nothing but the deadly vindictiveness of labor trouble accentuated by hatred toward the Negro."

The bloodbath drew the condemnation of other black activists as well, including Marcus Garvey. The head of the United Negro Improvement Association spoke passionately at a public forum in New York. "I can hardly see why black men should be debarred from going where they choose in the land of their birth," he said.

To go where one chooses was certainly an animating impulse for African Americans who abandoned places like Louisiana and Mississippi (where Ida B. Wells was born in slavery) for towns like East St. Louis, lured by fantastic tales told by relatives, the inventive lobbying of Pullman porters, and the promise of employers offering higher wages than a sharecropper ever dreamed of. But the Great Migration, its own kind of epic strut, was not without dead ends and hard reversals. Wells told the *Chicago Herald* that the labor unions of the North and the planters of the South were working together, using murder, arson, and intimidation "to drive the Negro back where he came from." Two steps forward, one step back.

Like Wells, the National Association for the Advancement of Colored People (NAACP) also pressed for congressional action, including an antilynching bill. In addition, on July 28, 1917, it staged the largest civic demonstration of its kind ever held before in the United States, a breakthrough display of collective strut. Ten thousand strong, black people marched along New York City's Fifth Avenue in a parade of protest. Men dressed in dark suits and straw boaters, women and children in white. Their expressions solemn and unyielding, they blazed a trail through public space, raising banners that announced their outright dissatisfaction.

**MR. PRESIDENT, WHY NOT MAKE AMERICA
SAFE FOR DEMOCRACY?
MOTHER, DO LYNCHERS GO TO HEAVEN?
YOUR HANDS ARE FULL OF BLOOD.**

Unlike the iconic mid-century marches that would follow, multiracial assemblies in which the heartfelt harmonizing of spirituals, civil rights anthems, and folk tunes provided a rousing chorus, not a song was sung. With the East St. Louis butchery still so fresh that they could almost taste the ash, the marchers stepped resolutely across New York City and never said a mumbling word.

The only sound was muffled drums.

> *It is absolutely necessary to the safety of this Province, that all due care be taken to restrain . . . Negroes [from the] using or keeping of drums . . . which may call together or give sign or notice to one another of their wicked designs and purposes.*
> —SLAVE CODE OF SOUTH CAROLINA (1740)

In choosing an instrument denied black people during their captivity, the NAACP was perhaps indulging in a bit of spiritual reclamation. The slaveholders' fear of drums bordered on superstition. They believed them capable of stirring up frenzy so contagious and fast-spreading that it was nearly impossible to resist. Ironically, their suspicions were confirmed in the early twentieth century, when jazz became a national fascination. Like lynching, it frequently brought whites together to entertain appetites often scorned in polite society. Then, as now, whites' interactions with African Americans and their culture reflected a perplexing conjunction of lust and disdain. Many white East St. Louisans, for example, may very well have been in their parlors listening with rapt attention to a recording of "Darktown Strutters' Ball" before going out to mutilate and murder their neighbors in nearby Black Valley.

Released less than two months before the massacre, the Original Dixieland Jazz Band's rendition of the song quickly ruled. Written by black composer Shelton Brooks, the tune interests me because it was among the first to introduce the black strut to a mass "mainstream" audience. An all-white combo, the Originals made their name, as it were, copying the black music developed in and around the Storyville district of New Orleans. (A 1917 record cover proclaims them "The Creators of Jazz.") The area's most notable native son was Louis Armstrong, whose "Struttin' with Some Barbecue" (along with dozens of his other tunes) also became a jazz standard. My favorite of his many versions was recorded in 1953, fifteen years after Joe Louis made mincemeat out of Max Schmeling, twelve years after Navy crewman Dorie Miller grabbed an antiaircraft gun and helped blast dive-bombing Japanese out of the sky, and six years after Jackie Robinson disrupted baseball with his Negro League panache. In a French film called *La route du bonheur* ("The Road to Happiness"), Armstrong and his All Stars blew with their usual pizzazz.

The set is made up to look like a street lined with bars and clubs. "Armstrong" blinks from a marquee in the background as the band assembles and quickly starts to play. Meanwhile, vocalist Velma Middleton cavorts among them with a baby carriage. The performance is at once rollicking and polished, with Armstrong's trademark trumpeting inducing in listeners an insistent urge to strut. Middleton's charms are evident but she never opens her mouth to sing, thus becoming a dark body whose purpose is purely ornamental. (Although one could imagine her as a proxy for Lil Hardin, Armstrong's second wife and, more important, the composer of the song). Watching the scene puts me at ease, as if my relatives at the family reunion suddenly sprang from their picnic blankets and revealed themselves as musical geniuses. Still, it's impossible to dismiss the band's mugging and what we might call extreme grinning, especially on the part of Armstrong and bassist Arvell Shaw. Radiating an unlikely exuberance that recalls the ruby-lipped caricatures on the sheet music of "Darktown Strutters' Ball," they stretch their faces to such an extent that it becomes difficult to distinguish a grin from a grimace. Are they mugging to make their brilliance more acceptable? Or could they simply be caught up in the ecstasy of making art? Their elastic expressions raise the specter of a judgmental audience lurking just beyond the frame. Unlike my experience watching Lil Buck dance, I can't watch Armstrong strut without phantom viewers threatening my enjoyment.

Lil Buck gets to narrate his own story, although it tellingly ends in the museum, where he has been alone the whole time. Our gaze supersedes that of the camera and perhaps even our double consciousness, enabling us to consider for a moment that our interaction with Lil Buck is unmediated. The noise of racially turbulent France fails to penetrate the museum's walls.

Unlike Lil Buck and Louis Armstrong, most of us can't trip the light fantastic or transform trumpet solos into miracles of sound and feeling. We are left to rely on others in the struggle to rouse our bodies and spirits into motion. When I stagger from my house still groggy with sleep, I turn to the generous gods of bop and groove to help me get my hustle on. I pop my earbuds in, press Play, and soon I'm walking down the street like Bernie Casey in *I'm Gonna Git You Sucka*, my theme music guiding my feet. My playlist is subject to the twists and turns of my fickle tastes, but some tunes never lose their favored status:

"Green Onions" by Booker T. & the M.G.'s
"Groove Yard" by the Montgomery Brothers
"Steppin'" by the World Saxophone Quartet
"The 'In' Crowd" by the Ramsey Lewis Trio
"The Sidewinder" by Lee Morgan
"Giant Steps" by John Coltrane
"Soulful Strut" by Young-Holt Unlimited

My playlist propels me through public spaces where my presence might be questioned or challenged. One August morning I was walking with earbuds firmly in place when someone called out to me. I turned and saw a white cop standing in the middle of the street, the sun glinting off his mirrored sunglasses. "You doing laps?" he asked. I told him I was.

"Which lap is this?"

"My second," I replied.

He gave me a thumbs-up. I nodded, unsmiling, and went on my way. I couldn't tell if he was just being friendly or letting me know that I was under surveillance. To ease my troubled mind, I pumped up the volume. I might even cautiously assert that I began to strut. In my case, that means walking with an exaggerated rhythm and rolling my shoulders as if they're too muscular for my clothing to contain, a misguided idea of masculine motion that I picked up during my impressionable youth. Most people who come from where I'm from refer to it as a pimp stroll, a nod to its preeminence in popular 1970s films like *The Mack* and *Hell Up in Harlem*—although I'm pretty sure Zora Neale Hurston was describing the same action when she wrote about slick New Yorkers "percolating" down the avenue in 1942.

I've seen brothers in Baltimore and St. Louis rock their

wheelchairs with a similar gangster lean, thereby converting the pimp stroll to a pimp roll.

You don't have to be a man to strut, although the typical heterosexual male imagination usually mistakes any other version for a favorable response to catcalling, a hip-swinging invitation to "take things to the next level." Freed from the default gaze, strutting is more likely to reflect the enchanting intelligence of human beings who know their power and maybe even revel in it. Janelle Monáe walking a tightrope while Big Boi chants encouragement? Strut. Ava DuVernay headed to the set of *Selma*? Strut. Valerie Jarrett strolling through the West Wing? Strut.

Sometimes we strut to reassure ourselves that we belong, that we have a right to the air we breathe and the space we occupy. At other times, we strut as if we could take back everything that has been lost. During a concert performance by New Orleans piano master Ellis Marsalis Jr., four of his sons, and bassist Roland Guerin, the players seem intent on reclaiming the decorum forbidden to Armstrong. As "Struttin' with Some Barbecue" begins, Branford Marsalis beams affectionately at his siblings. There is some moderate toe-tapping, knee-bending, and gentle head-nodding as the sextet methodically slays the song. But anything close to a smile is rare, and there is certainly nothing like the broad grins of Armstrong and Arvell Shaw. Their serious demeanor conveys confidence in their ability to let the music speak for itself. The audience yells enthusiastically but their gaze pales in importance to that of the benevolent yet exacting patriarch, overseeing his sons' artistry from his perch at the keyboard.

Watching a clip of the performance, I think of Strivers Row, the Talented Tenth, New Negroes sharing their work in a Harlem brownstone. I resist the urge to visualize the musicians playing the tune at their own backyard cook-out, dressed in jeans and sneakers while dinner sweats on the grill. It is perhaps a testament to their uncanny gifts that they manage to strut while mostly standing still.

Their ability to translate the raucous funk of Storyville while wearing neckties and stiff collars also testifies to the flexibility of strut, the way its boundaries shimmer and stretch. Offering further proof, Shelton Brooks has said he composed "Darktown Strutters' Ball" with denizens of the urban underworld in mind. According to him, the city's pimps and prostitutes held an annual event in which they discarded garb associated with their professions and dressed more like, well, an affluent jazz sextet. And even in the splendor of a concert hall we understand that "strut-tin' with some barbecue" doesn't mean taking a walk with a pulled-pork sandwich. Cab Calloway, keeper of the Book of Jive, defined "barbecue" as a girlfriend, a beauty. The song's insinuation is closer to the musings of the eminent philosopher John Lee Hooker. "Boom, boom, boom, boom," he sings. "Yeah, yeah, yeah, yeah. I love to see you strut." Profane or proper, haughty or naughty, strutting can be roomy enough to accommodate a low-down, foot-stomping blues *and* the dignified signifying of the Marsalis fam.

> *Stony the road we trod . . .*
> —JAMES WELDON JOHNSON,
> "LIFT EV'RY VOICE AND SING"

I wonder what songs would have been on Elizabeth Eckford's playlist? In 1957, four years after Armstrong and his All-Stars released "Struttin'" and decades before iPods,

Eckford found herself walking alone to Little Rock Central High. Separated from the eight other black students who would join her in integrating the school, she was forced to maneuver through a crowd of furious white women and men. They spat poisonous curses at her with all the enthusiasm of monkeys hurling feces at gawking humans. One could say those rabid Arkansans were in a prison of their own making, trapped in a destructive mythology, prevented from exercising their full humanity. One could almost pity them, if not for the impact of their psychosis on the black people then living in Little Rock. They could not sleep, eat, learn, or walk according to their own desires. I have long been intrigued by the famous photograph of Eckford strutting carefully through that corridor of shrieking flesh, her expression stoic, her books held close to her chest, her eyes hidden behind dark glasses. I'm amazed that she stayed on her feet, reached her destination with no bop or groove to drown out that loathsome chorus.

In contrast to Little Rock, it was mostly men who pushed and shoved a young black woman named Shiya Nwanguma at a Louisville Trump rally in Kentucky in March 2016. Video footage shows her assailants (including white supremacist Matthew Heimbach and an elderly Korean War veteran) jostling her and cursing her while Trump hollers "Get out!" from the podium. Like the predators of Little Rock, the feverish Kentuckians can barely restrain themselves in their eagerness to inflict harm on a black woman's body. Americans who recall the slave codes of yesterday may marvel, as I did, that those frenetic tribesmen assembled in the Louisville convention center were able "to give sign or notice to one another of their wicked designs and purposes" without the assistance of a single drum. All they needed was the urging of a bully with a pulpit. In both incidents (nearly sixty years apart), a black woman walked a solitary path with her life in danger, her own deportment a dramatic contrast to the uncivilized pack yelping and snarling around her. This is called strutting while holding body and soul together.

Richard Wright successfully argued that the Negro was America's metaphor; let us extend that notion to the situations Eckford and Nwanguma found themselves in. Their opponents—drunk on unfair advantage and absurdly imbalanced numbers—challenged their freedom to occupy, manipulate, and move through space, indeed their ability to take an independent step in any direction. On a larger scale, our former captors, similarly advantaged, frequently make a sport of denying us our basic human rights. When not pursuing physical punishment via overzealous policing, disparate sentencing, and mass incarceration, they debate our capabilities and subject us to their taxonomical impulses. Eckford's struggle to get to school leads me to envision black bodies moving through time unhindered by desperate talk of bell curves, crime genes, fast-twitch muscle fibers, and cultures of poverty. In such visions, I seek shelter from a white majority apparently inclined to limit us to a few options: glued to a slide like a lab specimen, working tirelessly on its behalf, comforting it with entertainment, caged up, silenced, or absent. While the narrowness of white desire can sometimes threaten to render our genuine selves invisible in an Ellisonian sense, it is also true that *perceived* blackness is never unseen. The imagined black presence boosts our population to impossible percentages while placing us at sites of white dysfunction where we haven't deigned to tread. From Charles Stuart and Susan Smith to Scott Lattin and Paul LePage, white people falsely implicating phantom black perps is a durable American tradition.

Perhaps the only thing that can challenge white fragility more than mythical fearsome Negroes is the disturbing sight of living, breathing black people gathering in one place by the thousands, their feet pounding the earth like those notorious drums. A. Philip Randolph's threat to organize a nationwide march of Negroes in 1941 was enough to frighten President Franklin Delano Roosevelt into integrating the defense industries during World War II. The implications of the 1963 March on Washington depended on one's perspective. With around 250,000 black people and their allies strutting through the nation's capital, it was either a dream realized or a nightmare come to life. Like the NAACP's silent march of 1917, it managed to sway the consciences of some white people while inflaming the hatred of others. It's no stretch to draw a dotted line from that march to the bombing of Birmingham's Sixteenth Street Baptist Church later that year.

While Washington had been the ultimate march by any measure, few if any observers thought it would be the last. Three months after Stokely Carmichael yelled "Black Power" during James Meredith's March against Fear from Memphis to Jackson, Mississippi, activists in Chicago took to the streets in nearby Cicero, Illinois. The suburb's infamous reputation had been cemented in 1951, when six thousand whites violently attacked a single black family, preventing them from moving in. On May 25, 1966, four bat-wielding white youths upheld community values by bludgeoning Jerome Huey to death. A seventeen-year-old black college student, Huey had gone to Cicero to apply for a job. He was on his way home when the thugs jumped him near the bus stop.

The sting of Huey's death was still lingering on September 4, when the Congress of Racial Equality (CORE) led two hundred marchers into Cicero to protest segregated housing. Three thousand white hecklers were waiting to greet them. "Go back to the jungle," they yelled while calling them "niggers," "black bastards," and other choice epithets. "The Zoo Wants You," one banner proclaimed. No one was seriously hurt, the *Chicago Tribune* reported, although there were several skirmishes. Cicero residents hurled bricks, bottles, and firecrackers. Some marchers picked them up and hurled them back.

Martin Luther King Jr. didn't participate in the march but spoke to a student group in Chicago that evening. "Some astronauts walked in outer space and you can't walk the streets of Cicero," he said. By then the civil rights leader had already learned that strutting could be as risky in the so-called liberal North as it was in the stubborn South.

In Cicero, Little Rock, and other hotbeds of manic segregation, racial wilding was often the province of civilians—unlettered white men and unfulfilled white housewives acting out their frustrations. In the twenty-first century, when strutting where one chooses is still seen as intolerable black impudence, police officers become gun-wielding surrogates. Licensed to kill, they can exorcise collective white hysteria by inflicting violence on our dark skins. In addition to satisfying a psychological urge, policing of the black body performs a critical economic function by supplying the nation's need for cheap captive labor and fodder for the prison-industrial complex. For these and other reasons, African Americans move through space fully aware of this fact: Police officers break the black body with the reliable blessing of the state.

Since Darren Wilson's killing of Mike Brown removed any doubt that an objectionable strut is grounds for murder, Black Lives Matter activists have marched in the path of their predecessors, challenging the popular compulsion to crush and consume blackness. Still the best service they contribute may be their expressed willingness to question the sanity of returning again and again to request protection and justice from a government that will not save us. The question reflects a perspective older than the republic, offered by Thomas Paine long ago: "Common sense will tell us, that the power which hath endeavored to subdue us, is of all others, the most improper to defend us." The bloodthirsty impulse—the desire to see the dark body suffer—shared by many of those who benefit from unfair advantage based on skin color may prove impossible to rehabilitate, a prospect that many of us are reluctant to acknowledge or confront.

In 1975, I was wowed by *The Wiz*. There was much to admire in the brilliant, all-black reimagining of L. Frank Baum's classic. My favorite characters had no memorable lines, no crowd-pleasing solos. Instead of Dorothy, say, or the Scarecrow, I was drawn to the Road. In Geoffrey Holder's Broadway staging, the famous Yellow Brick Road was embodied by a quartet of golden, nappy-headed brothers who escorted the main characters on their journey to Oz. George Faison's Tony Award–winning choreography combined the exuberance of the cakewalk with the flashy footwork of a Jackson Five performance, which the four dancers executed to the tune of "Ease on Down the Road." In the big-screen version of *The Wiz* produced three years later, director Sidney Lumet replaced the silent dancers with twenty-six miles of Congoleum. The film's disappointing box-office receipts can't be blamed on that single change, but it sure sapped the joy out of it for me. I think I found the Road dancers appealing because they reminded me of those smooth operators who bopped through our St. Louis neighborhood. In Big Apple caps, bell bottoms, and platform shoes, they looked as if they'd leaped out of those men's fashion ads in the back of *Ebony* magazine. I thought men who looked like that were the epitome of cool; free-range strutters whose knack for swagger extended beyond the block. Elegant and powerful, they were high-stepping, hip-dipping masters of the slide, the glide, and the insouciant saunter. I imagined they could go anywhere, even to the white side of town, and return with their black bodies intact. It was a fantasy, I realize, similar to the collective African American dream that we'll someday go from trodding James Weldon Johnson's stony road to easing on down it. It's a vision of a free black future that keeps us on our feet. Bodies in motion, we strut despite the persistent riddle of history, hard at our heels. We strut toward a future that is neither clear nor promised. We strut with consummate style. We strut with surpassing grace. We strut, therefore.

Justice will not be served until those who are unaffected are as outraged as those who are.

—Benjamin Franklin

SHOOTING NEGROES

Race came up again when the jury heard
four other phone calls to the police by
Mr. Zimmerman reporting suspicious
people in the neighborhood, all of them
black.

—Lizette Alvarez, *The New York Times*

When black people first set foot in the territory now
known as the United States, they stepped onto contested
ground. Before there was a legal term for what they were,
before the law carefully circumscribed their hearts and
loins, each of their footfalls was subject to contention.
How many strides until the end of their world? How far
could their limbs take them? To the edge of the plantation? To the back door of the big house? As far back as
the seventeenth century, long before Trayvon Martin took
his last steps in a gated community in Sanford, Florida,
his ancestors confronted similar boundaries. Gated neighborhoods? Try gated states. By the 1860s, several of them,
including Illinois, Indiana, Iowa, and Oregon, prohibited
black people from traveling anywhere without proof of
permission.

Your name?

George.

What's going on there, George?

I'm with the Neighborhood Watch, and we've had some burglaries and vandalisms lately. And this gentleman was walking in the neighborhood. And I've seen him before on trash days, going around picking up trash. I don't know what his deal is.

Is he white, black, or Hispanic?

Black.

Wherever such laws or customs prevailed, bands of dutiful citizens took on the task of enforcing them. Slave patrols, the forerunners of police cruisers and neighborhood watch squads, first emerged in South Carolina around 1704.

The patrols were based on earlier efforts in Barbados, where the Act for the Better Ordering and Governing of Negroes empowered all whites with the right to stop and investigate black people who, left to their own devices, were considered likely to steal or run away.

UP TO NO GOOD

In the view of patrollers, Negroes were as dishonorable as thieves. Consequently, they were to be apprehended and punished for moving or walking about without permission. In modern terms, patrollers were expected to be on the lookout for black people who were "up to no good."

Nineteenth-century black people wrestled with a dilemma in which "everything Negroes did was wrong," according to W. E. B. DuBois. "If they cowered on the plantations, they loved slavery," he observed. "If they ran away, they were lazy loafers." When everything they did was wrong, even something as innocuous as breathing could be cause for harassment or death. As Trayvon Martin discovered, twenty-first century racial maladies often pose the same trap.

"This guy looks like he's up to no good, or he's on drugs or something. It's raining and he's just walking around, looking about," George Zimmerman reported during his 911 call on February 26, 2012, moments before he gunned Martin down in cold blood. Zimmerman's easeful assumption of authority is both significant and historically resonant, but no more so than the notion that a black man simply walking—in his own neighborhood, no less—is automatically suspect.

Zimmerman's eagerness to take matters into his own hands reflects an implicit mandate that white citizens are as responsible for their safety as police officers are. Inheritors of a Patroller Complex deriving from those early acts for the better ordering of Negroes, they are, in effect, deputized to investigate any persons (read "black people") who seem out of place. When law enforcement officials speak to civilian groups, they seldom hesitate to reinforce this understanding. Following a highly publicized murder in Washington, DC, in July 2006, Andy Solberg, then-acting commander of the city's Second District, instructed a group of Georgetown residents to report anything suspicious—such as, say, the presence of African Americans. "This is not a racial thing to say that black people are unusual in Georgetown," he said. "This is a fact of life."

Solberg's language was only slightly more diplomatic than that of Sheriff Harry Lee, a notorious lawman who conducted an intrusive surveillance campaign against young black people in Jefferson Parish, Louisiana, in the

1980s. "If there are some young blacks driving a car late at night in a predominantly white neighborhood, they will be stopped," Lee promised. "There's a pretty good chance they're up to no good."

PIPELINE + PRISON = CHEAP LABOR

At least Lee's mythical troublemakers were driving a car; Solberg's scenario suggests that black people needn't do much more to deserve scrutiny than be seen standing on a corner or, to borrow Zimmerman's phrase, walking around and looking about. The idea that African Americans can commit a crime simply by existing is more than just a deeply entrenched racist misconception; it is also an idea rooted in capitalism's need for a cheap, exploitable labor force. These two barbed strands came together early in American history in the philosophy of prosperous landowners such as George Washington, who cast his practice of working slaves to death as a humanitarian gesture. Without constant work, he argued, they would be "ruined by idleness." Those strands can be tracked, as easily as a trail of spilled Skittles, to a modern prison-industrial complex that runs on equal parts racism and greed.

In the seventeenth century, forced labor was still something of an equal-opportunity injustice. States such as Connecticut and Florida arranged their prosecution and parole dockets according to planting schedules so that whites incarcerated in debtors' prisons could be conscripted to help with the harvest. They found themselves paying off their debt to society by toiling like slaves. The industry became less diverse after the Southern Rebellion, when Emancipation proved highly inconvenient for ambitious Confederate planters eager to shake off the dust of their inglorious defeat. Black Codes emerged, making criminal offenses of vagrancy, loitering, and public drunkenness.

> *There is [sic] two suspicious characters at the gate of my neighborhood and I've never seen them before. I have no idea what they're doing. They're just hanging out, loitering.*
>
> *Okay, Mr. Zimmerman, Can you describe the two individuals?*
>
> *Two African American males. They look uh, I know one is in a white Impala.*
>
> *How old do they look to you?*
>
> *Hmm, mid- to late twenties, early thirties.*

With the help of cooperative judges, black men and women unfortunate enough to be caught moving around, looking about, or even standing still in the wrong place at the wrong time were hauled back to the same fields where they previously sweated. (To get an idea of the durability of these underhanded practices, compare Black Code offenses with grounds for suspicion established during New York mayor Michael Bloomberg's stop-and-frisk reign of terror. They included "furtive movements," "fits a relevant description," and wearing "clothes commonly used in a crime.") Southern law officers, taking full advantage of the Thirteenth Amendment's timely loophole allowing compulsory labor "as a punishment for crime," set out to turn as many newly freed blacks into criminals as they could. States and counties filled their depleted coffers by convicting those they swept from the streets and leasing them to farmers and businessmen. Prison populations swelled, foreshadowing the incarceration disparities we see today—and a generation of "convicts" was sentenced to hard labor planting and harvesting crops, doing the most dangerous factory tasks, digging in mines, logging timber, and building railroads—ultimately laying the groundwork for the South's resurgent infrastructure.

Douglas Blackmon described the process in his Pulitzer Prize–winning book, *Slavery by Another Name*: "It was a form of bondage distinctly different from that of the antebellum South in that for most men, and the relatively few women drawn in, this slavery did not last a lifetime and did not automatically extend from one generation to the next. But it was nonetheless slavery—a system in which armies of free men, guilty of no crimes and entitled by law to freedom, were compelled to labor without compensation, were repeatedly bought and sold, and were forced to do the bidding of white masters through the regular application of extraordinary physical coercion."

PIPELINE + PRISON = PROFIT

Convict leasing, begun soon after the Southern Rebellion was crushed, officially ended in 1928, when Alabama terminated its program. Unofficially, states continued it under different guises. For example, in the state where Trayvon Martin breathed his last, prison officials added license plate, laundry, and shirt factories to their facilities after the state ended convict leasing. The practice continues today as a mainstay of private prisons, whose owners reap huge financial profits by using their inmates as low-wage and unpaid laborers. Companies such as CoreCivic (once named Corrections Corporation of America) and Geo Group owe their success to the American Legislative Exchange Council (ALEC), which they in turn sponsor through financial contributions. ALEC's work includes creating the template for the Prison Industries Act, a state legislation enabling the employment of inmate labor across the country. Just as Southern legislatures created Black Codes to establish a captive labor force, ALEC has abetted modern lawmakers' attempts to push through "three strikes" laws, mandatory minimums for nonviolent drug offenders, "truth-in-sentencing" laws, and anti-immigration measures designed to keep African Americans and Latinos off the streets and behind bars where, presumably, they'll be most useful. New agreements between state governments and private prisons can also include guaranteed minimum occupancy rates (see CoreCivic's purchase of Ohio's Lake Erie Correctional Institution in January 2012, for example), making "tough on crime" laws even more critical for profiteers of captive labor.

THE SUNSHINE STATE

Few states have followed ALEC's guidebooks more zealously than Florida, home of forty-eight state prisons, seven private prisons, and forty-one prison work programs. Black people make up 32 percent of the state's prison population, according to the Florida Department of Corrections, while making up around 16 percent of the state's entire population. In addition, at least one out of every five black people in Florida is banned from voting resulting from a felony conviction.

Unsurprisingly, Florida is the birthplace of Stand Your Ground (SYG), a law that most people weren't aware of until it was invoked—repeatedly—following Martin's violent death. With the help of National Rifle Association lobbyist Marion Hammer, Florida launched the law in 2005, empowering residents to use force to defend themselves against a perceived threat. Critics of such measures condemn them as Black Codes given a fresh coat of paint, but their complaints have mostly gone unheeded. Since 2005, ALEC and the NRA have helped more than twenty states add versions of the law to their own statutes. With SYG in mind on that rainy February night, the police permitted Zimmerman to do what law and custom made sure Martin could not: They let him walk.

> *Does he live in the neighborhood or is he just out walking?*
> *I don't know. It's the first time I've ever seen him.*

"A conversation about brutality and identity goes right to the body," the author and legal scholar David Dante Troutt has observed. The body, he goes on to argue, becomes "the currency of control." Consequently any discussion of black bodies, at least regarding their sojourn in America, must also include the idea of ownership. For black people to claim possession of their bodies, they must also declare themselves persons, capable of agency, language, and independent thought. Perhaps unsurprisingly, that humanizing impulse remains partly indigestible in a nation whose economic foundation depended on the idea that black people were not humans to be respected but property to be maintained. Property cannot be maintained if it dares to move about freely and—even worse—resists being apprehended.

BODY SNATCHERS

Solomon Northup's encounter with this dehumanizing process provides a useful example. In his 1853 memoir,

Twelve Years a Slave, he relates his first moments after body snatchers captured him in Washington, DC, and subsequently sold him into slavery. Awaking in darkness and in chains, he reached into his pockets "as far as the fetters would allow" and made another troubling discovery. "I had not only been robbed of liberty," he later recalled, but "my money and free papers were gone!"

Edward P. Jones portrays an ordeal no less horrifying for being fictional. In his novel *The Known World*, Augustus Townsend, a free black man, must sit helplessly in his mule-drawn wagon while a hostile white man takes Augustus's dearly purchased free papers and stuffs them into his own mouth. Augustus's wife is waiting for him at home, not far away. She might as well be in Africa as Augustus watches a white man devour his freedom.

As if speaking for all black people similarly abused, Solomon Northup bemoans his fate as a free American "who had wronged no man, nor violated any law" only to be "dealt with thus inhumanly."

Northup's experience and Jones's novel illustrate how even nominally free black people were nonetheless captives, vulnerable to the caprice and power of men of questionable integrity whom authorities endowed with the power to determine life and death. The state's peculiar permissiveness deputized half-wits to wreck lives with the kindly approval of the state. George Zimmerman's power to fire his licensed handgun at an unarmed teen and strike him dead with legal impunity lengthens a tradition of dubious deputizing that began in the slavery era and continued after Emancipation.

As Sally Hadden points out in *Slave Patrols: Law and Violence in Virginia and the Carolinas*, during Reconstruction lawmen and Klansmen adopted enforcement methods initially designed to monitor the enslaved. Together they turned patrolling into "a highly effective but still legal means of racial oppression."

Three factors combined to create a deadly environment for the newly emancipated: 1) battle-hardened white men with military training, 2) widespread fear of imaginary rampaging blacks hell-bent for revenge and white women, and 3) a marrow-deep belief that blackness and freedom are irreconcilable. From this strange brew the posse tradition emerged, extending the might of the law to volunteers who operated both with and without official sanction, depending on the circumstances and popular sentiment.

BULLIES WITH BADGES

"Posses, which were cheap, quick, and ruthlessly effective, provided welcome assistance to law officers," William Fitzhugh Brundage observed in his history of lynching in the New South. "Hence, posses and the violence they initiated endured in much of the South until at least the 1920s." And beyond. More than 4,000 black people were lynched between 1877 and 1950, usually at the hands of posses. Perhaps the most haunting demonstration of posse violence took place on March 7, 1965, a day now remembered as Bloody Sunday. Long before Sheriff Joe Arpaio and self-anointed "militiamen" began to troll Arizona's dusty perimeter for elusive undocumented Latinos, Sheriff Jim Clark conducted a similar campaign of terror against the black people of Dallas County, Alabama. Under his boisterously racist command, a posse of mounted Alabama state troopers and "volunteer officers" brutalized a group of peaceful protesters on the Edmund Pettus Bridge. While the protesters were unarmed, the posse was prepared for war. Their weapons included clubs as big as baseball bats, guns, bullwhips, and at least one rubber hose wrapped with barbed wire.

Tear gas, too. Mustn't forget that: C-4—a particularly toxic form of the gas—was designed to induce crippling nausea.

Activists John Lewis and Hosea Williams led the marchers. Fifty feet from the bottom of the bridge, a police major ordered them to stop and reverse direction. He gave them two minutes to comply.

"We couldn't go forward. We couldn't go back," Lewis remembered. "There was only one option left that I could see."

The men chose to kneel and pray. They passed the word but had hardly moved when the major issued his fateful order:

"Troopers! Advance!"

The mob of armed lawmen surged forward in an awful wave of malevolence, clubs and whips in motion. They descended on their defenseless opponents and, in a tradition as old as the country itself, commenced to dispensing justice American style, cracking skulls, crunching bones, and flaying the vulnerable flesh of men, women, and children.

"Something about that day in Selma touched a nerve deeper than anything that had come before," Lewis contends. "The sight of them rolling over us like human tanks was something that had never been seen before."

In many such civil rights movement skirmishes, posses rolled over marchers in full view of the federal government. Recalling another showdown in Selma, this one in 1963, activist historian Howard Zinn witnessed federal officials refusing to intervene on behalf of more than three hundred black people waiting to register outside the county courthouse. Surrounded by blue-helmeted troopers brandishing guns and cattle prods, some of the prospective voters had been standing in line for five hours or more.

Zinn writes, "I spoke to the senior Justice Department attorney: 'Is there any reason why a representative of the Justice Department can't go over and talk to the state troopers and say these people are entitled to food and water?' He was perturbed by the question. There was a long pause. Then he said, 'I won't do it.' He paused again. 'I believe they do have the right to receive food and water. But I won't do it.'"

John Conyers, a young attorney from Detroit who later became a congressman, was also on the scene. "Those cops could have massacred all those three hundred Negroes on line," he said to Zinn, "and still nothing would have been done."

DEPUTY DAWG

More than fifty years after Selma, Conyers's charge still resounds. The Southern-fried behavior of government, via Stand Your Ground laws and juries that wink at wayward vigilantes, suggests that violence against unarmed black Americans continues to take place with the consent of the state—and by extension, the governed.

My name is George and I live at the Retreat at Twin Lakes subdivision. I'm part of the neighborhood watch.

The American vigilante is an offshoot of the posse, a stalwart guardian of community virtue so moved by threats to his home and hearth that he must take matters into his own hands. Impatient with the pace of cosmic justice and his neighbors' heartwarming faith in holy reckoning, he knows his quarry is quick on his feet, too swift and evasive for plodding squad cars and donut-swollen patrolmen. It takes a real man to do a man's job and who is more up to it than him? Deputy Dawg straps up and hits the streets.

NAME: *Kel-Tec 9 mm PF-9*
CALIBER: *9 mm*
LENGTH: *6 inches*
HEIGHT: *4.3 inches*
WIDTH: *0.9 inches*
BARREL LENGTH: *3 inches*
PRICE: *$330–$390*
WEIGHT, FULLY LOADED: *18 ounces*
TRIGGER PULL: *5 pounds*
EFFECTIVE RANGE: *7 yards*

Hard chrome and hollow points, baby, he's ready to roll. This is the Wild West and he needs no stinking badge to prove he's a natural-born badass.

OK, and this guy is he black, white, or Hispanic?
He looks black.

There have been far too many break-ins lately, broken windows, and "assholes" trespassing on his peace. On one of his moonstruck patrols, someone will die, sprawled on a lawn, torn up from a bullet designed to expand and disrupt the body's soft insides. A few bleeding hearts might object, but security is seldom achieved without a price. Flyers distributed to residents advise them to call him, not the police, to report suspicious activity. "We must send a message that we will not tolerate this in our community," the flyers declare. Not here. Not on his watch.

Are you following him?
Yes.
Okay, we don't need you to do that.

Before Trayvon Benjamin Martin was evicted from his body, before the open-eyed husk of him cooled and stiffened on a grassy lot in Sanford, Florida, he was a child. The son of Sybrina Fulton and Tracy Martin, he was loved and is sorely missed. He had no criminal record. Like Solomon Northup, he had wronged no man, nor violated any law.

If not for his parents' persistence, he'd be like so many others, buried without inquiry and presumed to have died while up to no good. By the approach of Zimmerman's trial, the response in black communities across the country suggested that Martin was poised to become a martyr and a catalyst, joining historical figures such as Sam Hose and Emmett Till.

DEATH AND DISHONOR

Sam Hose, a black Georgia laborer whose confrontation with a white man ended in the white man's death, was tortured to death by a lynch mob in 1899. After the mob ritually dismembered Hose's body (W. E. B. DuBois later described the murder as a crucifixion), they arrayed his knuckles and toes in a butcher shop window to intimidate black people and titillate thrill-seeking whites. For DuBois, learning about the displayed body parts amounted to "a red ray which could not be ignored." He turned from a life of quiet scholarship to a long and extraordinary career as a public activist and intellectual, shaping the emergence of the NAACP and organizing black people throughout the African diaspora. Whereas Hose's horrific death is mostly remembered for its impact on DuBois's trajectory, Emmett Till's killing resonated via a photograph circulated in *Jet* magazine, for many years the nation's most popular magazine among African American readers. Till, a black teenager, was murdered in Mississippi in 1955. His executioners shot him multiple times, bashed his head in, and tied a cotton gin fan to his neck with barbed wire before tossing his body in the Tallahatchie River. *Jet*'s publication of the photograph added critical momentum to the burgeoning civil rights movement. Rosa Parks pointed to Till's murder as an incentive behind her refusal to give up her seat on a public bus, an act of defiance that launched the Montgomery Bus Boycott. "I thought of Emmett Till, and when the bus driver ordered me to move to the back, I just couldn't move," she said.

For many newly politicized Americans of color, Trayvon's killing became a galvanizing force in much the same way that the image of Till's battered corpse helped stir Parks and thousands of others to action. News reports by black journalists Trymaine Lee, Charles Blow, and others were distributed on Facebook, Twitter, and other sites. Social media campaigns followed immediately afterward, spawning marches on statehouses where Stand Your Ground is in effect, along with online petitions calling for charges against Zimmerman.

Like many of the most effective protest campaigns of bygone eras, organized black outrage, channeled through groups such as the NAACP, Color of Change, and the Dream Defenders, received critical assistance from equally motivated allies outside African American communities. YouTube videos and blog posts from white, Latino, and Asian Americans professing their support lifted spirits and influenced citizens who might otherwise have turned a blind eye.

But even as Martin moved toward an unforeseen prominence as a symbol of his nation's enduring inequities, he was also becoming something of a national joke. His parents, appearing before their countrymen as paragons of dignified suffering, had to watch as their child, who had been merely a junior in high school, was sacrificed on the altar of American psychosis. The indignities he suffered for the sins of his nation have been widely circulated on the Internet, the modern equivalent of the shop window that proved so pivotal to DuBois's repurposing. Like the knuckles of Sam Hose, Facebook and Tumblr photographs of young white males posing as dead Trayvon, sprawled amid Skittles and cans of ice tea, both demonstrated the depravities of the vanishing majority and raised the ire of otherwise complacent observers. Assaults on Martin's reputation flourished amid sick jokes on Twitter, including a nauseating flurry from Todd Kincannon, former executive director of the South Carolina Republican Party:

> Will karma find me as quick as it did Trayvon? Oh wait I make it past my 18th birthday. So I guess the answer is no.
>
> Hey what's the difference between Trayvon Martin and a dead baby? They're both dead, but Pepsi doesn't taste like Trayvon.

In addition to the caricatures and demonizing, an aggressive disinformation campaign substituted the image of Trayvon with that of another black boy, shirtless and aggressively posturing. Another deception followed in the form of a viral screed that inserted in Martin's place a picture of Jayceon Terrell Taylor, a muscular thirtysomething rap star who performs as The Game. Said one earnest citizen who posted the photograph of The Game on his Facebook page, "I am not trying to say this was a good shooting. I am not trying to say this kid deserved to die. I am saying the media in the USA is controlled by liberals who twist and distort what you see and hear in order for you to see things their way."

The motives of Greg Cimeno, twenty-two, and William Filene, twenty-five, are less clear.

The Floridians celebrated Halloween by dressing as Zimmerman and Martin, respectively. Cimeno wore a "Neighborhood Watch" T-shirt, and Filene, wearing a black-face mask and a blood-spattered hoodie, proudly showed off their costumes via social media. On a widely circulated photograph, Cimeno pretends to shoot Filene in the head.

Other Americans wore similar getups, evidence of the quasi-erotic thrill that blackface and the ritual reenact-ment of violent black death apparently provides. Whereas white Georgians—men, women, and children—gathered by the thousands to bear joyous witness to the butchering of Sam Hose, countless voyeurs can endlessly revel in the virtual killing of Trayvon Martin, secure in the anony-mous glow of their cell phones and computer screens. Seeking to profit from the controversy, an Orlando-based entrepreneur created a shooting target complete with a hooded figure, a package of Skittles, and a can of ice tea. He told reporters he sold out his inventory in two days, further proof of the durable link between capital, white rage, and commoditized blackness.

Following Florida's halfhearted prosecution of Zimmerman, Attorney General Eric Holder discussed the possibility of a civil rights lawsuit at the federal level, an unlikely scenario that, even if it happened, would leave SYG untouched. Three months after Zimmerman walked away a free man, the opponents of SYG had yet to achieve a significant reversal.

STILL CONFEDERATES AFTER ALL THESE YEARS

In late October 2013, the Senate held hearings to review SYG laws. With Sybrina Fulton looking on, Texas representative Louis Gohmert echoed the Confederate obstinacy of centuries past. "The idea that states are less intelligent or less able to discern their citizens' needs is a mistake of federal proportions," Gohmert said. His argument reduces the occasional loss of black lives to a regrettable but acceptable inconvenience, a small price to pay for public safety and the sustenance of state's rights. SYG is the Patroller Complex written into law, Confederate in spirit and always invoked with black hordes—the ultimate phantom menace—in mind. Elected officials like Gohmert are confidently representative of a consensus among their constituencies, an ethos perhaps most memorably articulated by the bard of the Magnolia State, William Faulkner. "If it came to fighting," he said, "I'd fight for Mississippi against the United States even if it meant going out into the street and shooting Negroes." Zimmerman, on the prowl for suspicious black people, stalked the Retreat at Twin Lakes according to a similar creed. Clearly Faulkner's defense of armed vigilantism remains fatally relevant today.

And what he said about the past not being past? That, too.

Sundays too my father got up early
—Robert Hayden, "Those Winter Sundays"

COLOR HIM FATHER

1

Like many African Americans, I found considerable joy in Barack Obama's historic victory. I saw his campaign as both a vindication of our long struggle for fairness and full recognition and as evidence that our society has indeed achieved a substantial degree of progress. At the same time, I joined other black men in regarding the elevation of one of their own to the most powerful position in the world as an opportunity to shine a spotlight on our strivings. In a culture in which the failings of black males are frequently—if not overly—exposed, we have become particularly sensitive to how we are portrayed. Amid fire-and-brimstone denunciations of absence and irresponsibility, those of us who are present and striving have often cried, *What about us?* If we're doing what we're supposed to do, we complain, we are often overlooked.

A few years ago, a black woman writer that I know wrote a piece in a national magazine urging black men to shuck their various dysfunctions and "go back home" to their wives. I called her and shared my objections to the piece, testifying that I returned faithfully to my beloved spouse and children every night, but she had little patience with my protests. "I wasn't talking about guys like you," she said. "My piece was aimed at the rest of y'all."

The rest of us, it seems, tend to steal the spotlight. Not that we want a prize or anything. Ten years before Obama's victory, Chris Rock famously and persuasively punctured the notion that black men should be praised for merely fulfilling reasonable expectations. Responding to an online essay in support of Black Fathers Week (a commemoration I had never heard of), one frustrated commenter echoed Rock's observations: "So now we should celebrate when people do what they are supposed to, or is that so uncommon in the black community that we need to declare holidays for that?"

Granted, a holiday would be a bit much, but we'd be grateful for mere acknowledgment. That's probably why some black men were peeved when Obama attracted criticism from some quarters when he appeared to denounce black fathers during a Father's Day speech at the Apostolic Church of God on Chicago's South Side, delivered six months after his inauguration. Too many fathers are missing, he said, "from too many lives and too many homes. They have abandoned their responsibilities, acting like boys instead of men. And the foundations of our families are weaker because of it."

Clearly Obama wasn't talking about all black dads; his criticism followed his praise of fathers who are "examples of success and the men who constantly push us toward it." But the specifics of his comments were obscured by the sound-bite nature of coverage that the speech inevitably attracted. Inside the church, the enthusiastic response to Obama's remarks appeared to be unanimous. It's quite likely that his audience recognized his criticism of wayward black men as part of the tradition of black leadership, differing little from similar comments by such notable figures as Martin Luther King Jr., Malcolm X, and Jesse Jackson. Perhaps they understood, as Obama emphasized, that his viewpoint was deeply influenced by his own experience as the son of an absent black father.

In his speech, Obama expanded his criticism to "imperfect" fathers of all backgrounds. "There are still certain lessons we must strive to live and learn as fathers—whether we are black or white; rich or poor; from the South Side or the wealthiest suburb," he said. Unsurprisingly, Obama did discuss the most dreadful consequences of growing up without a father. "We know the statistics—that children who grow up without a father are five times more likely to live in poverty and commit crime; nine times more likely to drop out of schools and twenty times more likely to end up in prison," he said. What resonated most for me was not his citation of these familiar maladies or his stinging condemnation of juvenile behavior but his references to his own fatherless upbringing.

While Obama and I both lead productive lives—and are both dedicated fathers married to beautiful, dynamic black women—Obama is motivated in part by his resolve, also noted in his Father's Day speech, "to break the cycle" of negligent fatherhood in his own family. In sharp contrast, I'm not breaking a cycle. I'm continuing one. My parents have been happily married for nearly seventy years. Both sets of my grandparents had marriages that were far from ideal but were sufficiently joyful to last more than fifty years. Fatherhood and a long, fruitful marriage were easy for me to imagine from an early age.

In addition to growing up without a father, Obama grew up in Hawaii, where the paucity of black men further complicated his childhood years. He had undoubtedly noted a similar shortage of black women, a lack that also impeded his absorption of valuable African American lessons. Still, as he recalled in *Dreams from My Father*, his need for masculine role models was often uppermost in his mind. "I was trying to raise myself to be a black man in America," he wrote, "and beyond the given of my appearance, no one around me seemed to know what that meant."

During my childhood on St. Louis's nearly all-black North Side, *everyone* seemed to know what that meant. Even if I hadn't been graced with the exemplary presence of my father, I had plenty of other mentors and models to benefit from. They included my grandfathers, uncles, coaches, and neighbors whose kindly interactions shaped my values and personality as much as the instruction I received at Farragut Elementary, the school less than two blocks from my house. Mr. Logan, the soft-spoken elderly man who lived in the second house from the corner, and Mr. Nash, the retiree who volunteered as a crossing guard at the intersection that I crossed twice daily, were among the men who took a fatherly interest in my safety and happiness—whether I deserved it or not. While the women in my community contributed mightily to my understanding of self-respect and the importance of respecting others, Obama's Father's Day remarks, specific as they were, led me to recall in particular my childhood exposure to the world of men and boys.

Down Vandeventer Avenue, a few blocks south of the corner where Mr. Nash reliably patrolled, music wafting from Pierre's Record Shop added a suitably funky soundtrack to our lives. Those were the days when songs like the Winstons' "Color Him Father" climbed the charts alongside the usual odes to romance, dancing, and sweet sexy things. The Winstons began their hit with an aggressive burst of drums, followed by rhythm guitar, a sweet flurry of strings, and a triumphant blast of horns. Finally, the lead vocalist eased in with his smoky tenor:

> *There's a man at my house he's so big and strong*
> *He goes to work each day, stays all day long*

Just as Obama learned about African American culture by watching young black people on *Soul Train* and emulating the black basketball players he watched on TV, I watched the men of my community come and go, and their behavior and attitudes inevitably—and positively—influenced my own. An ambient masculinity, as robust and nourishing as pot liquor, enriched the atmosphere; a young boy needed only to take a deep breath to inhale the wisdom in the air. To most of my peers, the profile of a neighborhood father would probably have involved a man in a work uniform of some sort. He most likely would have been a habitual smoker and fond of enjoying a beer after a long day at the job. (Meanwhile, residential segregation enforced a kind of labor-force variety seldom seen today. In my immediate neighborhood, engineers, custodians, cafeteria workers, and at least one judge could exchange greetings from their respective porches.) These men populated the viewing stands at the neighborhood park at Little League games, and used the same field themselves for softball contests on late summer evenings. On holidays, they barbecued and set off fireworks in the front yard while their kids oohed and aahed from the safety of the porch. Nearby, their wives, bright-eyed and vibrant, snapped their fingers to songs coming from the portable radio.

"Think I'll color this man father," the Winstons sang. "I think I'll color him love."

2

Because I saw my father every day, his presence was deeply imprinted on my consciousness. Even if he had been away for several days (and he never was), all I had to do was wander into the living room to refresh my memory. His self-portrait, rendered in oil on canvas, graced the living-room wall nearest the window.

The painting had been more of an artistic exercise than anything else. We'd all been the subject of his painter's gaze at one time or another. In fact, his pastel portraits of each of his children were among my mother's favorite possessions; they occupied places of honor on our walls. It only made sense that he'd also included himself in its expansive range. The self-portrait was also a visual document of my father in the years before my birth and so provided a glimpse of a version of him that I could only wonder at. This father had more hair, although it was closely cropped, and sported the debonair, pencil-thin mustache of a man-about-town, the kind of mustache I later admired on photographs of Langston Hughes, Ralph Ellison, and Albert Murray.

My father and I wear the same size shoes; beyond that our resemblances are few. I'm a little taller, substantially heavier with longer limbs, and my facial features bear the unmistakable influence of my mother's side of the family. But as a child, I always insisted to amused adult relatives that I looked like my father. When I was in first grade, I dragged my mother all over town in pursuit of my own pair of wing-tipped shoes, thinking that if I really wanted to be seen as my father's miniature carbon copy, I could start with the feet and work my way up.

In the portrait, my father's expression is confident, resolute. He stares straight ahead while showing just a hint of humor. I was fascinated to learn that he'd done the painting by studying his face in the mirror, beginning with the broad outlines and facial features before filling in the flesh tones—copper, sienna, raw umber—shade by shade. My father had always impressed me as having no vanity; I couldn't imagine him peering intently into a mirror under any circumstances other than when he was shaving. Still, the man in the painting recalled other, seemingly unusual images of my father, captured in a series of black-and-white photographs mounted on my parents' bedroom wall. Except in the wedding portrait in which my normally extroverted mom appears shy and even disarmingly demure, she looks dazzling in these shots, glowing and self-assured. Uncharacteristically, my dad seems very much her match and very much at ease as they pose at a nightclub, his rakish grin exposing his gold tooth. I'd witnessed fleeting glimpses of that side of my father on those occasions when he came home from a long day of teaching and sat down at the piano, his loosened tie dangling from his throat. He'd briefly forget himself as he exuberantly pounded the keys boogie-woogie style, belting songs like "Shortnin' Bread" and "You Can't Be Lucky All the Time." But, this was a side of my father I rarely saw, and it surfaced less as I began to grow up.

Since having been born way down in the birth order, I was used to a different kind of dad. This variety was a traditional head of household, a hardworking type whose disfavor was feared and whose laughter was savored. Who didn't go to nightclubs or taverns, but one who confined his pleasure-seeking to a can of cold beer and a ball game on the radio. A father who was friendly and witty and told us tall tales about a giant cat named Tabby while dressed in clothes that always evoked the world of work. My mother, who spent her days managing our home and all of us, was also a storyteller. Her style was a potent contrast to my father's, colorful, irreverent, and punctuated by exuberant bursts of laughter. She was outspoken where he was quiet, animated where he was still. Their partnership seemed based on a deep, mutual understanding and a willing acknowledgment of complementary strengths. Instead of inhibiting my father, her ebullience supported and encouraged him, and his comparatively reserved demeanor did the same for her. My father seemed more comfortable—and demonstrably affectionate—with her than anyone else, enjoying an easy intimacy that usually involved my mother sitting on my father's lap while he ate his dessert, with his collar unbuttoned and his tie askew.

My dad didn't shy away from disciplining us, although he tended to threaten more than anything else, and the threats were sufficient. "I'll wear you out," he'd growl while pretending to unbuckle his belt. My older siblings frequently reminded me that Dad had once been a much sterner figure, nothing like the grinning guy in the bedroom photographs. My sister swore that he used to inspect her room by running a white glove across each slat of her venetian blinds, but Dad just chuckled when I asked him about it.

Little by little, year after year, I composed my own portrait of my father. I mixed the colors on my palette not from memory or fantasy but from the fleshy reality of experience. The inveterate tinkerer who patched together our battered Rambler wagon with a few junkyard parts and elbow grease was the dad I knew best during my grade school years. In my primary grades, he taught me about homonyms and strengthened my vocabulary through countless games of Hangman. Once, when I was about six, he brought me to his class (he was teaching seventh grade then) to read aloud to the students so that they could see what "real" reading was. The year I turned twelve, we stayed up nights building a force measurer for science class, a blue papier-mâché elephant's mask for French class, and a zither for music class.

That same year, my father drove me to a nearby suburb several times a week and waited in the car while I practiced with a Little League baseball team. Watching my father reading *Popular Mechanics*, his black horn-rimmed glasses sliding down his nose, one of my teammates nicknamed my dad the motion-studies expert, a term we'd picked up from reading *Cheaper by the Dozen* in class. On the way home, we'd stop by Gateway Electronics, where my dad briefly morphed into a kid in a candy store, happily preoccupied with the glorious multitude of switches, motors, and gadgets.

The summer after seventh grade, I played organized baseball for the last time. My passion had waned even before the season ended, when I took to hanging out with my dad at the neighborhood tennis courts. Sometimes, we'd head straight to Fairgrounds Park without me even bothering to change from my Midtown Tigers uniform, so eager was I to trade backhands and forehands with him before it got too late.

I didn't realize it then, but tennis allowed me to spend

quality time alone with my father. Even though I was one of six, I never felt shortchanged in this regard. Somehow, despite all the other demands on his time, he managed to devote attention to each of his children. Sunday afternoons were his refuge, though. He'd spend most of the day at the park playing tennis with his friends, safe from the beck and call of his offspring. That is, until I started going to the park with him.

My dad had been an all-around jock. He lettered in multiple sports in high school, but didn't take up tennis until adulthood. By the time I joined him, we had already enjoyed many bonding experiences courtesy of our mutual interest in sports. My dad took me to my first major-league game, and always shared the sports section with me at the breakfast table. He seemed impressed by my ready command of batting averages and box scores, and I delighted in showing off. I nurtured my obsession with baseball the same way I pursued other interests: I went to the library. Soon I'd read all the relevant books in the Divoll Branch's young readers' section. I still remember plots and titles: *Little League Heroes*, *Soupbone*, and *Jake*, about a young black Little Leaguer whose father figure was Uncle Lenny, an itinerant musician.

I continued to play tennis regularly with my father, leading my team to the city's public high school championship while he coached a squad from a rival school. My best friend, whom I met in high school, has a dad much like my own. Hanging out at his house, I listened to his father's tales of growing up in the Deep South and studying at Hampton Institute. My visits to my friend's house supplemented my experiences at my home and in my neighborhood, adding another valuable component to the ambient masculinity from which I derived necessary sustenance. On one wall in my friend's house were framed copies of letters his dad had written to each of his children on the occasion of his or her birth. Many years later, my memory of those letters inspired me to write birth-day poems for my own children. My first reaction to those letters, however, was envy. I wished that my father, not an especially talkative man, could have expressed himself in such an open, vulnerable way. Eventually, I became aware enough to realize that my father's pastel portraits of us were letters too, that each stroke of pigment was itself an expression of paternal love and pride as eloquent as any line of verse.

Courtside, while we sat under the trees and discussed tennis strategy, my father talked as much as he ever did. I was old enough by then to understand and accept that he would never be as loquacious as some other dads. But, he shared tidbits about his life and thoughts, providing images that enabled me to construct my own portrait of him. I listened to anecdotes about the brief spell in his childhood when he and his siblings lived near a creek and his brother nearly drowned. I heard about the time his mother placed a pie on the windowsill to cool and a sudden rainfall seemed to ruin it. His siblings declined to eat the pie but my father was undeterred. As he recalled that pie while we sipped Gatorade and rested our muscles, my father all but licked his lips. "To this day," he said. "It's still some of the best pie I've ever had."

I learned about his various jobs—a child of the Depression, my dad began working at eleven. I had heard many stories at home reflecting his enthusiasm for teaching; nearly every day he regaled us over dinner with anecdotes about his students, full of humor and affection. So influential were these tales that three of his children grew up and became teachers themselves. At the courts, though, he often focused on jobs he'd held before devoting his career to education. I was especially fascinated with his recollections of working as a delivery boy for a drugstore while he was still in elementary school. He told me about the time he was surprised by a huge dog that stood on its hind legs and placed its front paws on my father's shoulders. Another time, a white woman to whom he'd just made a delivery smiled at him and said, "You're a good little nigger, aren't you?" Other times I learned about some of the things he ate when he was out with his friends, things my mother didn't serve at home, like pig ears, hot links, and tripe. Those were valuable life lessons for me: his work ethic, how he conducted himself, the way he honored his responsibilities.

When I left for college, my father was a rich and nuanced figure to me. In allowing me access to his interior, my father filled in the blank spaces, bringing his self-portrait up to the present. At the same time, he helped me to form my own complex identity. I had neither his facial features nor his wing tips, but I was made in his image nonetheless. He had molded me, although that fact had yet to sink in. But I knew enough to be grateful. Long ago, probably before I was born, my parents posted an anonymous poem on the wall in our house. They placed it where we'd see it each day as we brushed our teeth and prepared for school.

I took a piece of living clay,
And gently fashioned it day by day,
And molded with my power and art
A young child's soft and yielding heart.

I came again when years were gone:
It was a man I looked upon.
He still that early impress bore,
And I could fashion it never more.

Recently I stood in the room where that poem had been displayed. It was long gone, but I think of it still. I think of it and recall Sunday afternoons in the park, under the trees next to the tennis courts, listening to my father.

3

There's a nakedness in having the contents of one's life exposed. . . .
—Noelle Oxenhandler,
The New Yorker, August 7, 1995

Years passed. I went away to college, got married, fathered children, returned to St. Louis. All the while, my father soldiered on with his trademark quiet integrity.

My parents had lived in the same house for thirty-five years. They'd raised four boys and two girls. Their move to a much smaller house in a much safer, quieter, suburban neighborhood represented a sea change in the life of our extended family. Although five of us had long since moved out, the house on Sullivan Avenue had been the place where we regularly gathered. Most of us lived nearby and could arrive in a matter of minutes. My older brothers still had keys and came and went as they pleased. We all felt free to make ourselves at home, routinely raiding the refrigerator and dipping spoons into the pots that always seemed to be simmering on the stove.

Although we still enjoyed those same privileges at the new house, the atmosphere was different somehow. Warmth and love permeated the new premises sure enough, but the carefree atmosphere, the sense of sanctuary, had diminished. For one thing, the new house was tiny. It had two bedrooms, and everything was on one floor. For me the new house symbolized an unavoidable turning, a sense of crossing a threshold from which there could be no turning back. My parents seemed older, smaller. My siblings and I also seemed older, staring down middle age.

The opportunity to buy the old house seemed to be a chance for me to hold on to a little bit of a past rapidly achieving a patina of nostalgia, a thick layer of sentiment. It also represented more space for our growing brood. In April, my wife had given birth to Indigo, a beautiful daughter to go with our two handsome sons. Our rented two-bedroom flat was no longer big enough.

Ten months and countless frustrations later, we purchased the house. Liana and I boxed our books and papers while our contractor and his crew began loading in drywall at our new home.

But there was a problem: My father had never cleared out the basement.

My brother Guy pitched an idea: My three brothers and I would remove my father's belongings from the basement and carry them into the backyard. From there, my father could determine what he wanted to keep and what he wanted to discard. We'd load the desired things onto Guy's truck; the rest would be trashed.

When I got to the house at 9:00 a.m., my brother Seitu

had already arrived. He was in the backyard taking a look at my mother's old garden. Nearly a year had passed since my parents moved. The garden, no longer controlled by my mother's constant care, was beginning to grow wild. Garlic was everywhere, its bulbs extended from the long stalks like antennae of some strange, extraterrestrial beast. Blackberries were in abundance too, rich, ripe, and redundant. The thick lawn was a combination of sturdy zoysia and clover blossoms browning in the summer heat. We went to work in earnest after Guy showed up.

For many years, my father had supplemented his schoolteacher income by moonlighting as a sign painter. He often worked in the basement, part of which was partitioned into a studio for him. I have fond memories, more imagined than not, of "working" beside him, scratching out rudimentary letters with my own paints and brushes while he painted glorious pit-roasted pigs for Q King Barbecue, or multicolored horoscope signs for Ruby's Zodiac Lounge. But, he didn't just paint signs. His Cubist painting of a guitarist hung over our couch during my childhood, and his hand-carved hardwood mask graced an adjacent wall. Both pieces made the move to the new house, as did the beloved pastel portraits.

Over the years, as Dad's passion changed from painting to electronics, he became an expert builder of speaker cabinets, amp kits, and various kinds of stereo gadgetry.

My dad built me a pair of speakers to take to college with me, and they became cherished companions through countless moves. Just as my father had captured my impish toddler grin in his pastel portrait of me, I made various attempts as a young poet to fashion an image of him in verse. I usually began with his passions. Visualizing him bent over his worktable, peering through the thick lens of a magnifying lamp as he touched a soldering iron to a transistor's tiny tendrils, I imagined him prying secrets from the circuitry.

if you could
you surely would
see inside the science of sound,

track the transit
of silence-slicing signals
as they

burst out as music
through woofer, tweeter & midrange
past crackle & hiss

to decibel-dance on air . . .

In time, my dad's private portion of the basement gradually expanded to take over the whole area. Thirty-five years' worth of possessions made it difficult for anyone other than my father to make it past the stairs and navigate the narrow pathways piled high with speakers, tools, rolls of canvas, empty frames, and rows of art paper.

Stacked in the basement, my father's things were part of his private life, with an emphasis on private. As children, we seldom penetrated his lair. Usually, we hovered near his door until our queries drew him out. Eventually, he'd emerge, dusty, preoccupied, happy. Guy, Seitu, and I began lugging stuff up the exterior basement stairs to the backyard. Shortly afterward, Boyce showed up. He's the youngest by far, born six years after me. Guy and myself are only three years apart while Seitu, now deceased, was ten years older than me. In those days, Seitu and I were roughly the same size. Guy, although a little shorter, was much thicker, and years of working with his hands had made him quite solid. Boyce was the tallest and most powerfully built, with thick wrists like the barrels of baseball bats. We worked quickly, spicing our labor with the jokes and small talk of easy camaraderie. Yet, I wondered if, like me, their laughter hid deeper thoughts. Were they also still curious about this man who raised us, loved us, taught us so many things?

The backyard was nearly filled when my father rolled up the alley in his station wagon. I think we all felt a little apprehensive when he opened the back gate and walked in, surveying the results of our labor. He was clad in his customary khakis. Never a large man, our father was summer-slim, older, slower. Yet, cords of veins still rippled along the insides of his nut-brown forearms.

Strewn on the lawn were the bits and pieces of our father's private passions: motors, circular saws, a jigsaw, buckets of brushes, stacks of silkscreens, old gym bags stuffed with tennis balls, speaker cabinets, old fiberglass insulation, old ropes, three vacuum cleaners, four washing machines, handsaws, old lamps, dusty sketchbooks. It was like sifting through a dead man's things, except our father was alive and breathing and eyeing each piece with longing. Still, it was a wake of sorts. In the end, he took only a few items, some tools, a speaker or two, some things that had belonged to his own father.

Would I someday relive this scenario with my own sons? Would I eventually choose a few things, some of them things that had belonged to my own dad, just as my dad had done before me?

We agreed to meet again the following Sunday. The sky grew gray and drizzle began to fall, gradually growing into heavy rain. It seemed appropriate somehow.

Years have passed since that day in the yard. My wife and I were blessed with two more sons. We moved from my childhood home and raised our brood far from our Midwest origins. My father is nearly ninety, weakened by ailments and the cruelty of time. I see him far less often than I would like, less often than I imagined. I have had the opportunity to discuss Obama's victory with him, and have been thrilled to share in his delight and surprise. I hope that future remembrances of Father's Day will continue to provide occasions for African American men to not only discuss and debate our shortcomings as fathers but also to pay tribute to the tradition of paternal accomplishment that also winds its way through our public and personal histories. I hope we will step forward and sing the praises of well-known men as well as the kind of men Obama briefly mentioned at the Apostolic Church of God, the ones who are "examples of success and the men who constantly push us toward it." Doing so will not distract us from other problems that beset our communities, factors such as persistent systematic racism, economic inequality, and cops who menace our blocks like gangsters with badges. After all, it's not an either-or situation. We can identify issues and work toward solving them while also casting a brief spotlight on men like my dad, whose steadfast toil amounts to a legacy of sturdy labor and reliable vigilance, of sacrifice and guidance—of what my wife would call coverage. My father, like the central figure in Robert Hayden's "Those Winter Sundays," got up early and "made banked fires blaze." Quiet and self-effacing, he was always uncomfortable with effusive displays of affection. He'd likely react similarly to any suggestion that his life—his fatherhood—merited any special mention. He'd say that he was just doing his job.

He'd be right, of course. But failing to honor those who do right threatens to consign them to the same sketchy outlines inhabited by absent fathers, and threatens to wash away their images as steadily as the rain that fell on my brothers and me amid the assorted fragments of my father's life. It is that prospect, however unlikely, that inspires me to tell my own children about Dad's childhood adventures and the lessons he imparted beneath the shelter of a tree. It keeps the memories fresh and vivid, enabling me to dip into them whenever the copper, sienna, and raw umber start to fade. Then I can touch my paintbrush to the palette, and color him in again.

The whole world opened to me when I learned to read.

—Mary McLeod Bethune

THE SEER AND THE SEEN
ON READING AND BEING

In 1965, *Saturday Review* published a groundbreaking essay, "The All-White World of Children's Books." Its author, Nancy Larrick, lamented the enormous racial imbalance in books for young readers. Her survey of 5,206 books published in a three-year period showed that fewer than 7 percent of them included images of African Americans. "Of the books which publishers report as 'including one or more Negroes,'" she wrote, "many show only one or two dark faces in a crowd. In others, the litho-pencil sketches leave the reader wondering whether a delicate shadow indicates a racial difference or a case of sunburn." A former president of the International Reading Association, Larrick warned that the huge preponderance of white-centered children's books could distort white youngsters' understanding of their place in the world. If they grew up without encountering numerous and varied representations of people of color, they might not ever learn to see things as they are.

She also considered the impact of the disparity on young black readers. "In Cleveland," she wrote, "53 per cent of the children in kindergarten through high school are Negro. In St. Louis, the figure is 56.9 per cent. . . . Across the country, 6,340,000 nonwhite children are learning to read and to understand the American way of life in books which either omit them entirely or scarcely mention them. There is no need to elaborate upon the damage—much of it irreparable—to the Negro child's personality."

Larrick exaggerates the fragility of young black psyches, but I take her point. Literature written with African American children in mind doesn't replace the many other ways in which collective wisdom and affirmation are conveyed from generation to generation (including music, art, and the instruction of elders). Instead it complements those sources, strengthening the narrative framework that helps us make sense of the black experience.

Two years after her essay appeared, I entered kindergarten as part of that expanding black student population she had noted in St. Louis. Of the children's books I'd seen up to that point, I don't remember many that included kids who looked like me. The one exception had been Watty Piper's *Gateway to Storyland*, which included an unremarkable version of "Little Black Sambo" that steered clear of stereotypes, at least as I recall it. That changed in 1968 during a field trip to our city's main library. Under the watchful eye of our teacher, Mrs. Hayden, we first graders sat attentively while a librarian read to us from *Oh Lord, I Wish I Was a Buzzard*. It was newly published that year, and the (white) librarian may have been eager or even delighted to welcome an audience that seemed ideally suited for it. Written by Polly Greenberg and illustrated by Aliki, it's a spare, poetic picture book about a family of African American sharecroppers tasked with harvesting an immense field of cotton. Aliki limited her palette to browns, muted oranges, hints of gray, and white space imaginatively used. The opening image reveals the sun hovering above stalks of long brown grass. On the following page, a man and his two children set out for the fields. Father and son wear overalls and floppy straw hats; the daughter, barefoot, wears a striped kerchief and a simple dress. The monotony of the setting is offset slightly by the lovely patterns on their clothing, but there is little vibrancy otherwise. The color purple will never pop up among these rows.

None of the characters smile as they work. The family picks and gathers in the foreground; behind them, backs bend in the distance. The cotton often appears as white blots, infinite and demanding, as if the artist flung them at her canvas. The sun remains close overhead as the story progresses, radiating above endless waves of undulant bolls.

Greenberg's text used repetition effectively to drive home the drudgery and discomfort of the family's work. "We picked and we picked / and we picked and we picked," the girl regularly reminds us. "It was hot, oh my, it was hot" runs through the narrative like the chorus of a Delta blues.

Aside from the principal characters, the figures are rendered in telling fragments; we see only shoulders, backs, hats, and elbows. The cotton could almost be seen as devouring or slowly digesting them. Near the middle of the book, Aliki used tricks of perspective to show cotton stalks looming on the horizon as tall as trees.

The unnamed narrator, accustomed as she is to menial chores, searches for amiable distractions. She envies the freedom of every animal she sees. "Oh, Lord, I wish I was a buzzard," she says, wiping her brow.

The freedom of the bird, a nearby dog, and a fluttering

butterfly seem to taunt her as she toils, reminding her (and us) of her family's relative confinement. To my adult eyes, the animals' ability to roam or rest at will underscores black people's demeaned status at the bottom of the Jim Crow ecosystem, tethered to the land even though their chains are gone. In contrast, as a first grader, my eyes marveled mostly at the girl's brown skin, her loveliness and her resemblance to the women and girls who populated my world. She notes that they finished "on Saturday," concluding not a day but a week of hard, tedious labor. Her father rewards his children with lollipops. Only then do the girl and boy get to smile and behave like youngsters.

Part of what made *Buzzard* special was Mrs. Hayden's visible enchantment with it. At first, I thought she paid rapt attention because she wanted to model proper behavior for us. But soon, it became clear that she'd almost forgotten we were there. If a children's book about a little black girl was novel to us, I'm now imagining what it must have meant to her, not just as a dedicated educator who had worked with all-white textbooks for decades but also as a mature black woman who was once a little black girl. I thought none of that, then, of course. Still, I found her enthusiasm catching. I no longer recall if Mrs. Hayden borrowed the book from the library right then and there, or later ordered it from a bookstore. I just remember that only a few days seemed to pass before a copy appeared in our classroom. Mrs. Hayden read it to us with unbridled joy. It may seem odd that a book that offered an unblinking look at child laborers sweating under a broiling sun made a classroom of restless first graders so happy. It was a testament to the book's quality, perhaps, as well as its timely fulfillment of a hunger that maybe we didn't even know we had. We had seen some version of ourselves, and that absorbed us enough to keep us sitting still.

That field trip was not my first visit to the library. My father had taken me there to obtain my own library card shortly after I turned five. With his help I checked out a book about Noah's Ark (I don't remember the author, only its small, toddler-friendly dimensions and its dull yellow cover) and *Circus* by Dick Bruna, wonderfully bright with thick cardboard pages. It was the beginning of a long friendship with libraries that included even a brief stint of employment when I was a young man and newly wed. I worked my way through much of Philip Roth's output while shelving large print books at the Community Services department in St. Louis, and sold my first newspaper article while working there. For the princely sum of thirty-five dollars, the *St. Louis American*, a black weekly, bought my interview with a legally blind sculptor. My wife, Liana, was working two part-time jobs at a downtown mall on the day the article published. During our lunch breaks, we hurried toward each other on a street halfway between our workplaces. I remember her holding the *American* above her head like a banner as she advanced, her grin as bright and dazzling as the moment when she first caught my eye.

Bookmobile visits began in first grade. While the huge library on wheels parked directly on the blacktop playground of Farragut School, we formed orderly groups and filed in and out. This was the year before my baseball obsession began, at which point my reading choices seldom strayed from books about the national pastime. I do remember working my way through Beatrix Potter and becoming particularly enamored with *The Roly-Poly Pudding*.

My subsequent attachment to all things baseball may be the cause of my missing *Who Look at Me*, a children's book published in 1969, when I was in second grade. It had begun as a collaboration between the authors Milton Meltzer and Langston Hughes. The latter's death in 1967 put the project on hold until Meltzer enlisted the poet June Jordan to take it over. Meltzer had assembled a collection of paintings and illustrations, some by noted African American artists such as Charles Alston and Henry Ossawa Tanner; others came from white painters like Colleen Browning and Alice Neel, known for their sensitive renderings of black life and culture. The images encompass many aspects of the African American experience, including street scenes, formal family sittings, children at play and adults at work. Jordan's words, musical and formidable, function much as a choir would; as the pages turn, the voices she assumes become a collective shout of assertion, an impassioned demand for recognition and acknowledgment.

"We only see what we look at," John Berger wrote in *Ways of Seeing*. "To look is an act of choice." In the grip of Jordan's words, readers may regard the summons to gaze as both an exhortation and a dare, less an act of free will than a surrendering to the inevitable pull of forces beyond their control.

> *see me darkly covered ribs*
> *around my heart across my skull*
> *thin skin protects the part*
> *that dulls from longing*

In echoing Ellison, Jordan places blackness, complex and unpredictable, in the center of the frame. At the same time, she tenderly considers the risks of visibility, how speedily the spotlight can be turned into crosshairs. Fifty years before Freddy Gray would die after making "eye contact" with a policeman, and Philando Castile's noticeably "broad nose" led to his execution, Jordan limned the high-tension wire between the seer and the seen.

How would I have felt about *Who Look at Me*? The poetry, brilliant to my grown-up eyes, may not have been accessible to my seven-year-old self. I was familiar enough with art. My dad was a fine artist and a sign painter when not teaching. He often took us to the museum on Tuesday nights when admission was free. Along with my brother Seitu, he had helped create our community's Wall of Respect, a mural/gathering spot where poets and revolutionaries shared their musings and manifestos before sizable crowds. Indoors, my father made his art in his basement studio or at a nearby sign shop. My brother drew wherever he was—even while in motion, from the kitchen to the dining room, from the backyard to the front porch. He spent countless hours teaching me how to color. Two years later, when I was nine, he would be out of the house, a married father with new responsibilities. In the meantime, we met on a bench near the heating vent in the front hall. As we dug our fingers into a Dutch Masters cigar box, searching through dozens of stubbed and broken crayons, we worked on coloring books featuring Gumby and Pokey and a short-lived cartoon series called *The Super Six*. Seitu transformed his pages into textured, layered, and shaded portraits, often rubbing the paper with his fingers to create the proper blend, say, of cornflower blue and forest green. While scribbling beside him, I struggled to stay between the lines.

Outside our house, I seldom saw figurative art with black bodies. *Who Look at Me* would have held my interest for that alone. I must say, though, that my house and my neighborhood had no shortage of black bodies, and while I couldn't say for sure whose gaze I attracted, everyone and everything attracted mine. The streets shimmered with personalities as rich, mystifying, and dynamic as those captured by any work of oil or watercolor. To the extent that I recognized my neighbors as reflections of myself (and as children we understood this instinctively), I could look out my window and see "me" everywhere I turned.

Aside from *Buzzard*, I can remember only one other book in my first-grade classroom with a character that looked like me: *Two Is a Team* by Lorraine and Jerrold Beim. The story of a friendship between Ted, a black boy, and Paul, a white one, it unfolds predictably in workmanlike prose. Ted's presence initially drew me to the book, but after a while I became more interested in the images of the two pals visiting each other's homes. This was the same year that the beautiful black actress Diahann Carroll starred in *Julia*, a TV show in which her son, Corey, had a similar friendship with Earl J. Waggedorn, a white classmate. When Ted and Paul played with a sailboat while Ted's lovely mother sat nearby, it reminded me, pleasantly, of Corey and Earl. The pedestrian text seldom matched Ernest Crichlow's brisk illustrations. Although I don't remember doing so, I'm sure I read the promotional copy on the jacket flap introducing Chrichlow as "a distinguished young Negro artist." I didn't learn until decades later that he was indeed reputable, an active member of a generation of painters that included Romare Bearden, Jacob Lawrence, and Norman Lewis.

A far more lively book was Ezra Jack Keats's classic *The*

Snowy Day, which I borrowed from the library, but I don't remember seeing in my first-grade classroom. It was published in 1962; *Two Is a Team*, astonishingly, was published back in 1945. Taken together, Mrs. Hayden's bookshelf and Nancy Larrick's exhaustive research suggest that little else was published during the years in between.

In Mrs. Hayden's class, picture books were reserved for story time or quiet reading. For serious study, we turned to *Jack and Janet*, part of Houghton Mifflin's Reading for Meaning series. Here is where my father's schoolteacher background provided me with an advantage. Most of the books in the series, including *Up and Away*, *Come Along*, and *On We Go*, were on a shelf in our house, residuals from Dad's end-of-semester classroom clean-outs. I finished them at home while Mrs. Hayden was still leading us through the pages of *Jack and Janet* in class. I was fond of the title characters, as well as their little sister, Penny, their pets Tip and Mitten, and their pals Bill and Dot.

> *Put **m** with **eat***
> *and you have **meat**.*

> *Do you eat meat?*

> *Put **b** with **eat***
> *And you have **beat**.*

> *Who will beat Jack home?*

People of color—and the racial "problems" that usually came with them—did not exist in the pastoral paradise where Jack and Janet lived. While they might occasionally encounter a stray goat or kitten, no Negro would ever stop and ask for directions or show up on the porch looking to rent a room. Difficulties usually stemmed from a harmless misunderstanding, easily resolved within the span of a few pages. Rereading *Jack and Janet* as an adult, I was struck by the authors' awareness of changing gender politics, as well as their uncertainty about how to address them.

In one typical adventure, a new boy, Dick, tries to trade a pocketknife for Tip, Jack's beloved dog. But Tip also belongs to Janet, so she will have to consent to the exchange. She turns her nose up at the pocketknife. "That is not good for a girl," she says. "A girl could not play with it." Janet reconsiders when Dick offers to add a tricycle to the bargain. "A girl could play with that," she says.

In a subsequent episode, Penny suggests buying Jack a pair of dolls for his birthday, but Janet says, "No! Put those back. Those are good for girls but not for boys."

Janet buys Jack a kite instead. Later he declines to let her and Dot help him fly it. "Kites are for boys," he tells them. "Kites are not for girls."

Janet and Dot win the argument by successfully flying the kite after Jack has tried and failed. They tie the kite string to the baby carriage in which they are pushing a doll.

"It is a good kite for girls," Janet says. But, she might have added, only if they agree to mind the children at the same time.

*Take the **l** away from **look**.*
*Put in **b** to make **book**.*
What do you do with a book?

Jack and Janet served as the color bearer, as it were, for the rest of the Reading for Meaning series. *Come Along* consisted of original stories and abridged adaptations of popular picture books such as *Curious George* and *Katy and the Big Snow*. Aside from the figures in "The Five Brothers," an adaptation of a Chinese fairy tale, every character in its 250-plus pages was white. *On We Go*, which I absolutely loved, featured a cameo by a different quintet of Chinese men. Besides them, the book's only acknowledgment that people of color exist occurs when a white man entertains his kids by allowing them to paint his face with red stripes like "a big Chief." The only principal character with brown skin is a dog named Noodle.

Notwithstanding Nancy Larrick's dire forecast, I found the world conjured in those books more fascinating than alienating. I enjoyed every moment I spent there, but I never considered for a minute that it was better than the nurturing, stimulating all-black world to which I would return after shutting the book.

I take mild umbrage with Larrick's prediction of "irreparable" harm because it cast a pall of hopelessness over the black readers she aimed to defend. Much like a presidential candidate who solicits black voters by asking them what else they have to lose, she may have encouraged her readers to see black communities as quagmires of hopelessness, and black people as suffering from terminal illiteracy and dysfunctional vocabularies.

I don't pretend that our family household was typical, but I am confident there were others like it. Born the fifth of six children, I grew up in a culture of reading. Some days I could hardly wait to get older, when I stood to inherit my siblings' libraries. My eldest sister Dale's shelves held books by Baldwin and Hemingway, among others. With little effort, I can still see her Scribner's paperback edition of *The Old Man and the Sea*. Seitu had stacks of Marvel comics and an almost complete set of Doc Savage adventures, most of which I eventually snapped up. My sister Karen collected Nancy Drew and Hardy Boys mysteries, all of them hardbacks. In time, I would start with *The Secret of the Old Clock* and *The Hidden Staircase*.

My older siblings neither marveled at my precociousness (not out of place in our household) nor condescended to me. When I was about thirteen, Karen, observing my boredom with books designed for readers my age, began to share her own. From a pile of thrillers she had been racing through, she tossed me *The Chancellor Manuscript* by Robert Ludlum. "It has some sex in it," she said, "but you can handle it."

Reading material was always at hand throughout my extended family. My paternal grandparents subscribed to *The Crisis* (the official publication of the NAACP), my maternal grandfather kept piles of *Black Enterprise* in his bedroom and allowed me to take the back issues home to read at my leisure, and my parents subscribed to both daily newspapers as well as *Ebony*, a widely circulated African American magazine. *Jet*, *Ebony*'s immensely popular sister publication, could be found in every barbershop, beauty salon, and record store. That said, perhaps our community's best resource was our muscular imaginations. They were not in short supply in black neighborhoods across the country, where storytelling remains a spectator sport. Some of us may not have had many books, but we all had plenty of stories.

I don't mean to suggest that having a rich oral tradition

is the same as being literate. Our teachers were instructed to make sure we knew the difference, as well as the connections. It was to this combined legacy of creativity and literacy that I turned when I began to write children's books myself. I was not responding to any lack that I experienced as a young reader so much as aiming to sustain the tradition that had nourished and enlightened me.

The revised edition of *Oh Lord, I Wish I Was a Buzzard*, published in 2002, includes a note from Polly Greenberg, recalling her work creating Head Start centers in Mississippi during the 1960s. It was there that she met Gladys Henton. "The story in this book is based on a childhood recollection" of Henton's, Greenberg explains.

In another book, *The Devil Has Slippery Shoes* (weighing in at a whopping eight-hundred-plus pages), Greenberg wrote in considerable detail about the poor, black Mississippians she came to know while working in the Magnolia State. Gladys Henton doesn't appear in those pages, but Hattie Saffold does. She parlayed her experience as a Head Start instructor into a college degree and a career as a kindergarten teacher. Her memories show that Gladys Henton's experience was far from unique.

We raised some cotton, some corn, vegetables, a few hogs, cows, chickens. My mother and father were farmers. We lived near them. For survival, we had to work on plantations, too, chopping cotton for about $3 a day in that hot, hot sun, or picking—$2 for a hundred [pounds of cotton. It takes over half a day to accomplish this, so this also paid $3 a day]. When our children were small, I'd drop them off up the road at

my mother's, but when they got a little bigger, they'd
come along and work too. We needed every dollar. . . .
We were getting about $45 a week for the full-time
work of two adults and a bunch of kids, and it was
seasonal.

Buzzard offered a realistic and even unpleasant view
of life seldom—if ever—reflected in white children's literature published at the same time. In her afterword,
Greenberg suggested that young readers be told that the
story "took place before their mothers were born." Yet
Saffold describes children toiling in the fields as recently
as 1965, when the War on Poverty brought funds and jobs
to the state. My mother-in-law, born in Robinsonville,
Mississippi, in 1946, managed somehow to avoid setting
foot in a cotton field until she was a teenager. "It would be
hot," she told me. "You had a big hat on and a thermos of
water. You put your sack across your shoulder, you pick it
and put it in the side. When you get to the end of the row,
you tie it up and leave it there. A man drives by in a trac-
tor, gets it, weighs it, writes a number by your name and
brings your sack back. My first day I picked 280 [pounds].
I picked 280 to 310 every day."

And how much was she paid? "Three dollars a hundred," she said.

After reading the original edition of *Oh Lord, I Wish I
Was a Buzzard*, my mother-in-law attested to the accuracy
of Greenberg's narrative. Still, she was struck more by the
heroine's resourcefulness than by the endless drudgery.
"She never got disheartened because in her heart she knew
she was doing what she had to do to survive," she said.
"She's very observant. She notices everything while constantly doing her work and keeping her purpose in mind."

I asked her if it was possible to experience joyful moments in the field, and she quickly assured me it was. "It was hot but it was also pleasant. Sometimes my sister Jenny and I would take a boll of cotton and throw it at each other. Mama would shake her head because she knew my stepdad wouldn't like that."

Like nearly every other first grader in Mrs. Hayden's class, I had my own not-so-distant connection to cotton and to Mississippi. I knew that my mother's father had been born there. I didn't know, however, that my enslaved ancestors had toiled in Amite County, where much of the state's cotton had been cultivated.

Most of what I later learned about conditions in antebellum Mississippi came from studying *The Slaves of Liberty*, a book by the fine historian Dale Edwyna Smith, who happens to be my sister. Tireless and determined in her pursuit of our ancestral legacy, she sifted through archives, traveled to Mississippi, interviewed descendants, confirmed connections, reexamined details, and verified hunches. I find reading about historians' efforts to get at the truth—the U-turns, dead ends, and gravity-testing journeys across rope bridges—as satisfying as learning about the history they eventually uncover. The details of searches like those Greenberg and my sister conducted easily impress someone like me, whose idea of adventure involves a cool drink and a comfortable armchair.

My sister's essay in the *Southern Review*, published in 1990, reconstructed the story of Irris Bonner Harris, born in Amite County around 1856. During a research project, Dale came upon Irris unawares "in the pages of a book at Harvard's Widener Library." While reading

WPA interviews with the formerly enslaved, she writes, "I felt sure that I was looking at words inspired by my own flesh and blood." Her essay travels back to the past from its starting point in 1950, when as an infant, she was carried to McComb, Mississippi, to be blessed by our family's matriarch, one Irris Bonner Harris.

Through the magic of modern software, I can download a photograph of their fateful meeting and look at it on my smartphone. The picture is a miracle of genetics and circumstance, five generations of my family in a single portrait. In the right foreground, Dale sits on my mother's lap. A teenage bride, my mother sparkles with girlish beauty. My grandfather stands behind them, his hand on my mother's shoulder. My great-grandfather, tall and dignified, stands in the background on the left. In front of him sits Irris, relaxed and regal. If there is Mississippi in her face, I don't see it, although I don't know if I'd recognize it if it were present. Similarly, her face tells me little about her childhood in bondage, her chronically injured hip, or the sundry ordeals that must have marked her ninety-plus years. I can, I think, see evidence of the amusements she had enjoyed and the loves she had known, the sweet surprises and the joy. Her expression is alert and her lips are turned slightly, as if suppressing merriment.

From my sister, I learned about the inadequacies of census-taking and transcriptions, the countless flaws in methodology that can undermine the historian's quest. Even if perfect, those kinds of documents couldn't provide the intangibles I crave, like the sound of Irris's voice, and the signature gestures that belonged to her alone. Neither can the photograph, for all my efforts to read and see it. For all I know, when my daughter lets loose her marvel-

ous chortle, it could be the echo of Irris's laughter, reso-
nating through the years.

The WPA interviewer who recorded Irris's recollections couldn't resist adding her own two cents to the narrative, or perhaps she was expected to. At any rate, positing
herself as a close observer, she concludes her report by telling us what (she thinks) she'd seen. Irris, she wrote, was a
"bright yellow . . . darkey who wants to be 'looked up' to."

My mother was born in St. Louis, but spent most of her
childhood in Sacramento, where she attended integrated
schools and enjoyed friendships with Latino, Asian, and
white classmates. Although returning to her rigidly segregated hometown as an adolescent had required some ad-
justment, it didn't prepare her for the sojourn to Mississippi.
My parents' trip to McComb with Dale was their first
journey to the Deep South, and their last. I had heard the
account of my parents' Mississippi pilgrimage many times.
Over the years, my mom had repeated a story about stop-
ping at a restaurant for a takeout meal soon after they'd
arrived in the state. Years later, the details eluded me. All
I could recall was my parents being sent to the back door
of the restaurant to await their food. When I called my
mother and asked her to repeat the story one more time,
she was eighty-six years old. More than sixty years had
passed; the details eluded her, too. Besides spending time
with the family matriarch, my mother most remembered
wanting to hurry back North and stay there. "I didn't like
Mississippi at all," she told me. "People deserve respect, especially adults. You should be careful how you talk to
people. They didn't care." Even over the phone, I could hear
the tension in her voice and imagine her furrowed brow

as she probed the gauzy details of her past. "It was the wrong place for somebody who's outspoken," she concluded. "I was about to get hurt down there. It wasn't my type of deal. I went because my daddy wanted me to go."

I worked at the *Washington Post* in the late nineties and early aughts. Once, while waiting for a meeting to start, I mentioned my formerly enslaved great-great-grandmother to my colleagues. I told them she had lived long enough to hold my sister on her lap. A fellow editor stared quizzically, looking not at me but just past my shoulder. With the fingers of one hand he tapped the fingers of the other, like a third grader solving a math problem. "Are you sure? That doesn't seem possible," he said, looking down at the table. It had happened and there was supporting evidence, but I knew he wouldn't be able to see it. His skepticism reddened his pale skin and emitted from him in waves, like body odor. "You can read all about it in the *Southern Review*," I said with no small degree of satisfaction. We left the matter unresolved, and he likely forgot our exchange by lunchtime. I still recall it from time to time, and when I do I also think of a passage in "The Law," a poem by Eugene Gloria:

> *What with those men and their gift*
> *of whiteness, their constant need of proof.*

At first glance, the only difference between the original and revised editions of *Oh Lord, I Wish I Was a Buzzard* seemed to be the author's explanatory afterword. When I looked again, however, I noticed a change in the way the little girl introduces her family's mission.

1968:
My daddy told us
if we didn't pick a lot of cotton
we were going to get a whipping.

2002:
My daddy told us
if we picked a lot of cotton
we might get a sucker.

Apparently, Greenberg or her editor thought the prospect of bodily harm might have been too much for twenty-first-century sensibilities. Gladys Henton likely wouldn't have mentioned the threat of a whipping if it were not a real possibility. Even so, Greenberg wasn't obligated to produce a verbatim reconstruction of actual events. A story "based on" someone else's memories leaves plenty of room for contraction and expansion. What's more, the searing heat and the backbreaking repetitiveness of the family's tasks make it more than clear that they weren't enjoying "a fun day" in the sun. In the original version, the father still holds out the possibility of a sucker, but only after he has first raised the possibility of punishment.

As has been pointed out many times, modern-day youngsters are exposed daily to violence through so many outlets that they risk becoming desensitized to it. My first-grade classmates, of course, had no access to video games, the Internet, or cable television. Still, it is likely that none of us blinked at the mention of a whipping. At my school, kids were beaten daily with yardsticks, rattans, hands, belts, and bolo bats. One girl's mother came to our class several times and disciplined her daughter on the spot with what she fondly called "the Persuader," a menacing, serpentine cord that she uncoiled from her purse with undisguised delight. As bad as a whipping from a teacher was, discipline from an administrator was much worse. Once Mr. Overton, the assistant principal whom we all feared, came into our classroom and ordered our class clown to bend over a desk. He whipped him ferociously with a bamboo pointer. The boy looked distressed but to my amazement he endured each blow without shedding a tear or uttering a cry. I nearly passed out—and I was sitting on the other side of the room.

In the slave narrative my sister had found, our ancestor spoke of the constant threat of violence as her mother and fellow captives labored among the cotton. "Marse Alex wud . . . ride ober de fiel' he all de time toted dat whip," she said, "an' sum times would pop it 'cross sum body's back." Returning to *Buzzard* as an adult, I found that the new knowledge stemming from my sister's research had colored my reading. History, lead-footed and relentless, weighed down the text. Nor was I able to see the illustrations as I once had, before I asked my mother-in-law to distill her experience into dollars and cents. While unquestionably a liberating force, at times reading can remind us of the limits of perception, the complications of looking.

Nancy Larrick must have had such complications in mind when she wrote her landmark report. She died in 2004, at age ninety-three, with the world of children's publishing only slightly more diverse than when she first examined it. There is little evidence to suggest that industry stalwarts paid serious attention to her warning about children's books that falsely positioned white characters at the center of the universe. She predicted that white youngsters raised on a steady diet of such books would grow up to become adults who'd have difficulty seeing people of color as peers, neighbors, or friends. I'm reminded of her gloomy forecast whenever my wife quietly signals me to offer my business card. It's a practiced routine of ours in settings where credentials might be helpful in explaining our black presence. Liana, all incandescence and grace, turns on her megawatt smile. I lead with my business card to ward off skepticism, holding it in my left hand while I lean in to shake with my right.

The recipient looks at the card, then up at my face, although the card has no photograph, only my name, a title, and contact information under my college's corporate logo. I've performed this ritual enough to sense when my new acquaintance is caught in a strange kind of dissonance, reading one thing while seeing another. At such moments I find myself also thinking of John Berger. "The relation between what we *see* and what we *know* is never settled," he wrote. "Each evening we see the sun set. We know that the earth is turning away from it. Yet the knowledge, the explanation, never quite fits the sight."

All
worship the Wall.

   —Gwendolyn Brooks, "The Wall"

BRICK RELICS

My wife, Liana, and I were driving through Medford, Massachusetts, on our way back to our home just outside Boston. Looking out the passenger window, I saw a low brick wall, short, straight, and parallel to the road. I thought little of it until I saw a sign that read "The Slave Wall." We drove by so quickly that I wasn't sure exactly what I'd seen. After we got home, I typed "slave wall" and "Medford" into an online search engine.

My writing practice normally involves plastering the walls around me with layers of paper, each splattered with simple sketches, stick figures, and nearly indecipherable scribbles. But, the wall in my new space is made of exposed brick; pushpins are impossible, and tape fares almost as poorly. The adhesive tries and fails to sustain a connection; sheets of paper curl and slide slowly to the floor like the last leaves of the season. Unfazed by these difficulties, I downloaded a color photograph of the wall I'd seen. I applied tape to the corners and pressed it to the bricks.

In the photograph, the wall looks about three feet high and twenty feet long. Its surface is so weathered that the individual bricks are no longer detectable in some places, obscured by white sediment or mortar crumbled to dust. It looks sturdy nonetheless, able to withstand wind, rain and, as it turned out, 250 years of history.

A man named Pomp built the wall in 1765. He was one of forty-nine enslaved black people in town at the time, according to the Medford Historical Society.

Medford was once the brickmaking capital of the Northeast. The area was rich in clay, the main ingredient, and brickyards sprang up to supply the bustling market in Boston and other New England towns. The industry was more than one hundred years old by the time Pomp set to work with his string line and trowels. Some of the town's most prominent citizens had stakes in the business, including members of the Tufts, Blanchard, Bradshaw, and Brooks families.

It was the Brooks tribe that pressed Pomp's bricklaying skills into service. At the bidding of his captor Thomas Brooks, he built the wall to mark the edge of the family's estate. I imagine Pomp kneeling with his tools, surveying the site while above him Brooks explains the project to a fellow capitalist. Everyone should know where one man's property ends and another's begins, I hear him say.

"Runagate Runagate," Robert Hayden's immortal poem, begins as a breathless sprint. It follows a group of runaways as they navigate by the stars and pursue freedom via the Underground Railroad. They flee "from darkness into darkness," away from hunters, hounds, and posters calling for their flesh.

If you see my Pompey, 30 yrs of age,
new breeches, plain stockings, negro shoes;

More than five thousand black people were held captive in Massachusetts when Pomp built his wall. Did he ever dream of escaping Brooks's clutches, to turn runagate and plunge into the dark?

In New England as in the South, captains of industry often burdened their enslaved human beings with ironic names that mocked their lowly circumstances. The cabins in the quarters were full of prophets, heroes, generals. Hence Abraham, Hercules, Pompey.

Pompey (106–48 BC), Roman general and statesman;
Latin name Gnaeus Pompeius Magnus; known as
Pompey the Great. He founded the First Triumvirate,
but later quarreled with Julius Caesar, who defeated
him at the battle of Pharsalus. He then fled to Egypt,
where he was murdered.

"Scratch a name in a landscape," the physicist and naturalist Chet Raymo has written, "and history bubbles up like a spring." In Medford, that history would pour forth dark and fast-rising, quickly eclipsing the height of Pomp's wall.

MEDFORD ENSLAVED CIRCA 1776

Worcester | Pompey | Rose
Pomp | Peter | London
Selby | Prince | Punch
Flora | Richard | Dinah
Caesar | Scipio | Peter
Nice | Cuffee | Isaac
Aaron | Chloe | Negro Girl
Negro Woman

Perhaps Pomp's name was shortened to distinguish him from the other Pompey. Or maybe his captors were just having more fun with language.

pomp: ceremony and splendid display, especially at a public event.
ORIGIN Middle English: from Old French *pompe*, via Latin from Greek *pompē*

Not much else is known about Pomp. He was likely long dead by 1792, when enslaved black people in Washington, DC, were forced to assist in the construction of the original White House. In a 2012 children's book called *Brick by Brick*, Charles R. Smith Jr. details their labors. Supported by Floyd Cooper's poignant illustrations, Smith keeps the text simple. "Rented as property, slave hands labor as diggers of stone, sawyers, and bricklayers," a typical passage reads.

Although that episode from our past had already been accessible to any eight-year-old with a library card, apparently it had been a secret kept from many adults. Michelle Obama laid it bare during her speech at the 2016 Democratic National Convention. "That is the story of this country," she said. "The story that has brought me to the stage tonight. The story of generations of people who felt the lash of bondage, the shame of servitude, the sting of segregation, who kept on striving, and hoping, and doing what needed to be done. So that today, I wake up every morning in a house that was built by slaves. And I watch my daughters—two beautiful intelligent black young women—play with the dog on the White House lawn." Certain conservatives, including a low-watt loudmouth on cable TV, denounced her as a dishonest race-baiter. Earnest journalists eagerly pursued the story, salivating at the prospect of the First Lady being caught in a lie.

The White House Historical Association backed her assertion. Its website reports that DC commissioners had difficulty recruiting construction workers and soon "turned to African-Americans—both enslaved and free—to provide the bulk of labor that built the White House, the United States Capitol, and other early government buildings." The whole kerfuffle should make clear that when black people say, "We built this nation," we are not dismissing the substantial contributions of others. We simply know that if we don't keep repeating it, blowhards and know-nothings will rush in with erasers at the ready. Our insistent demand for credit honors every black captive who dug stone, nailed planks, and stacked bricks, the Unknown Builders of decades past.

Hidden in plain sight, our ancestors' constructions offer a historical record of black lives in America that documents often can't. Pomp's wall, for example, predates by nearly one hundred years the first US census that listed black people by name. These testaments to African American craft and resourcefulness gain symbolic power against a twenty-first-century backdrop of resurgent racism and obsessive attachment to Confederate memorials. The genius of these builders endures not only in walls but also in domes and obelisks and intricate ironwork—even when their names do not.

At the unveiling of a quite different wall two hundred years later, Gwendolyn Brooks commemorated the occasion with a poem. Her lines included these:

> *It is the Hour of tribe and of vibration,*
> *the day-long Hour. It is the Hour*
> *of ringing, rouse, of ferment-festival.*

I sometimes think of those lines when I think of Pomp. Was he present at Thomas Brooks's Hour of Ringing, when the lord of the manor unveiled the grand entrance of his estate to his assembled tribe? Did anyone raise a toast to the bricklayer's dependable talent?

Vitrified Brick—In the past, a small dark "nigger brick" was used for the vitrified work in brick sewers, but recently the price in paving culls has been so attractive that they are used universally for this purpose. These brick[s] have been rejected on street work for some irregularity of form.

(W. W. Horner, "Sewer Construction in St. Louis,"
Engineering & Contracting, September 13, 1911)

If Pomp of Medford built the wall, why isn't his name
on it? Why is it called "The Slave Wall" instead? How much
more powerful the historical marker would be if it read
something like "Pomp was here. He deserves your respect."

*In the opinion of the court, the legislation and histo-
ries of the times, and the language used in the Declaration of Independence, show, that neither the class
of persons who had been imported as slaves, nor their
descendants, whether they had become free or not,
were then acknowledged as a part of the people, nor
intended to be included in the general words used in
that memorable instrument. . . . They had for more
than a century before been regarded as beings of an
inferior order, and altogether unfit to associate with
the white race, either in social or political relations;
and so far inferior, that they had no rights which the
white man was bound to respect. . . .*

(Justice Roger B. Taney, *Dred Scott v. Sandford*,
1857)

The sting of Taney's emphatic dismissal of black
people's basic human rights persisted for more than a
century; its residue still lingered during my childhood,
when civil rights bills were still being enacted. Not long
after I entered elementary school, Aretha Franklin transformed our long-fought quest for *respect* into a soul-
stirring anthem of personal autonomy. The lessons of
Freedom Summer still resounded, and liberation was in
the air. The uniform of protest had switched from suits

and church dresses to dashikis, medallions, and towering Afros. Hands clasped in prayerful supplication gave way to fists thrust defiantly skyward. "We Shall Overcome" was supplanted by "Black Power!" Reflecting the spirit of the age, inner-city muralists echoed calls for dignity and self-determination, expressing demands that went unsaid, perhaps undreamed of, in Pomp's day. Wielding brushes and buckets of paint, artists mounted ladders and scaffolds to splash color onto bricks until the stubborn masonry yielded. Poets, warriors, and philosophers bloomed into view. Hence Phillis, Malcolm, Douglass.

The mural movement took shape in 1967, with the dedication of the Wall of Respect on the South Side of Chicago, where Gwendolyn Brooks helped ring in the changes with "The Wall," her poem written for the occasion. In his poem of the same title, Don L. Lee (Haki Madhubuti) also saluted the twenty-foot-by-sixty-foot "mighty black wall":

> A black creation
> Black art, of the people,
> For the people,
> Art for people's sake
> Black people . . .

Murals began to spring up in other cities, including Detroit and St. Louis. In 1968, a group of seven painters including my father and eldest brother met in front of a wall at the intersection of Leffingwell and Franklin Avenues. Working with the support and protection of the Zulus, Black Liberators, and other activist groups, they adorned the bricks with portraits of H. Rap Brown, Phillis

Wheatley, W. E. B. DuBois, and other notable figures. They added a sign emblazoned with Marcus Garvey's famous exhortation, "Up, you mighty race." The wall became a gathering spot. Rallies convened regularly, complete with speeches, poems, and musical performances. Residents of the all–African American North Side were invited to black culture meetings every fourth Sunday of each month.

I have only a dim memory of events at the wall. The details are limited and perhaps not entirely accurate. A framed photograph of the mural, prominently displayed in my mother's living room, helps to fill in the blanks. It's a reproduction of an image originally published in the October 13, 1968, edition of the *St. Louis Post-Dispatch*, under the headline "Black Pride." When I study it certain memories return, or at least I think they do: the sight of my father and brother on ladders, the sound of crowds and music, the feel of my mother's hand holding mine. In my mind, the faces on the bricks seem as vivid as the day they were painted.

I look at the mural, at Wheatley, born in West Africa in 1753, and then to DuBois, who died there 210 years later. Between them, I see a shimmering filament of resource-fulness and determination, the invisible cable that connects our past to our present. I note that time has not been kind to every person depicted on the wall; some have lost their relevance or luster in the years since the newspaper published the photograph. Even so, that fact in no way removes them from the company of Makers and Doers and Artists who continue to shape the story of our experience here. Together they compose a narrative of epic resilience from clumps of earth, bits of wood, and permutations of brick.

Chastened by yet another brutal New England winter, we've postponed returning to Medford until we're certain of spring's arrival. Our pilgrimage there will be the most recent in a series of similar excursions. Of late, we have spent a long, hot afternoon in a Newport, Rhode Island, cemetery, looking for tombstones carved by the enslaved artisan Zingo Stevens. We have staggered through aggressive winds and eight-degree weather to pay respect to the fallen captives interred in the African Burying Ground in Portsmouth, New Hampshire. I suspect these trips do for me what churches or mosques do for many others, because they summon in me a close approximation of religious feeling. When I think of "religion," I think not of gods but of ancestors. My thoughts, I believe, have nothing to do with blasphemy and everything to do with sanctity, gratitude, and grace. Of principles embodied, foundations laid, and sacrifices endured. Dred. Fannie. Rosa. For me, they and others are the holiest of ghosts. The sight of Emmett Till's casket or a meeting hall, where Frederick Douglass shook the walls with his eloquence, moves my spirit more than talk of mangers, burning bushes, and parting seas ever could. In my embrace of these lives, these relics, I am saved by history, if only for a while. I have been blessed to discover that salvation may turn up in the unlikeliest of places, even by the side of a road in New England, where a man named Pomp built a wall.

You've taken my blues and gone
— Langston Hughes,
"Note on Commercial Theatre"

THE THING ITSELF

1

"This story ain't just about me."

That's Willie Dixon talking. He was a bassist, a blues legend, and an unofficial writer-in-residence during the heyday of Chicago-based Chess Records in the 1950s and '60s. Despite prison stints as a young man, Dixon managed to steer clear of most of the pitfalls that brought down many of his gifted peers, thus remaining on the scene for enough years to prosper—or, at the very least, actually receive royalties from the truckload of hits he composed. As portrayed by Cedric the Entertainer, he's the narrator of *Cadillac Records*, a 2008 film about the journey of African American music from Southern cotton fields to living rooms, jukeboxes, and concert halls around the world. Cedric speaks those words and plays Dixon as equal parts rascal, sage, and self-deprecating wizard. His delivery of Dixon's lines brings to mind one of my favorites among Cedric's comic creations: an assembly-line veteran who expertly diagnoses ailing cars while dangling a cigarette from his lip. (Such men were mainstays in the St. Louis neighborhoods where both Cedric and I grew up.)

Like Dixon says, the story is far from his alone. Other important musical figures receive significant screen time in the film, including brooding, brilliant Muddy Waters (Jeffrey Wright); broad-shouldered, barrel-chested Howlin' Wolf (Eamonn Walker); and the hyper, dapper Chuck Berry (Mos Def). Adrien Brody holds his own as Leonard Chess, the label's slick, hustling founder, and Beyoncé Knowles provides a melancholy turn as the charming, sexy, and deeply troubled Etta James. For me, the most riveting performance is that of Columbus Short as the mercurial, doomed harp prodigy, Little Walter.

More than any other form of music, songs created by African Americans have supplied the soundtrack to our nation's rich, imperfect unwinding. Just how much we have contributed has often been a matter of dispute because we have seldom had a commensurate hand in shaping the chronicle of our own genius. Darnell Martin, writer and director of *Cadillac Records*, seizes the reins of that narrative by telling the story via Dixon's wise, empathetic gaze. A seasoned observer and participant, Dixon offers commentary that suggests to the audience, "You may have heard other versions, but this is the way it all went down." His account includes instances of exploitation, imitation, and outright theft; all themes that continue to resonate amid present-day debates about cultural appropriation and African American creativity.

Darnell Martin's presence at the helm of *Cadillac Records* makes it a relative rarity among mainstream movies: a dramatic story about blackness, as it were, written and directed by an African American. While that fact is no guarantor of excellence, it increases the probability that blackness will occupy center stage instead of stagnating in the margins and the background. In Martin's hands, blackness flourishes not only in the music of her main characters but also in the gestures and rituals of their everyday lives. It shines, for instance, when Muddy Waters pauses from his sidewalk strumming to look up into a nearby window, where Gabrielle Union's breath-stopping beauty glows above him like a benevolent sun.

The director took artistic license here and there, as filmmakers often do. Phil Chess, Leonard's brother and business partner, doesn't exist in Martin's telling, and Bo Diddley, another of the label's famous musical pioneers, is similarly absent. These departures from the historical record are excusable (she was not making a documentary, after all) and become easier to overlook amid the film's successful, respectful handling of the spirit-infused African American ethos. It's a black thing, some might say, and she understands.

By ethos I mean the distilled experience of black life in all its myriad subtleties; a Jes Grew stew of sights, sounds, memories, movements, and emotions marinated in blues, swing, bop, soul, funk, gospel, and rap; a deep-blue blackness beyond category and bred in the bone, so high you can't get over it, so wide you can't get around it, so low you can't get under it. So insurmountable, it would seem, that merely attempting to define it inevitably diminishes it. The fact that blackness can incorporate such things as technique, practice, and the conscious application of style while simultaneously transcending all those things makes it nearly impossible to pin down. As a result, it often infuses American life as more of a tantalizing abstraction than a concrete attribute, some intangible quality derived from black people's history not on this continent but on this planet. Anyone who's seen the Norfolk State marching band, a New Orleans second line, or three black girls turning double Dutch knows what I mean.

Ralph Ellison touched on it when he described singer Jimmy Rushing's ability to give voice to "something which was very affirming of Negro life, feelings which you really couldn't put into words." When trying to wrap my vocabulary around blackness I find myself reduced to opaque mumbling. I want to say that I may not be able to describe exactly what blackness is but I know it when I see it. Or hear it. Or feel its irrepressible rhythm urging me to get on my good foot and dance my way out of my constrictions. Blackness as a timeless, undeniable force simmers at the heart of every African American story and, by extension, nearly every American saga. However, its tendency to elude description complicates our claims of ownership.

Complications become further entangled when culture gets converted to commerce, as Martin makes plain in *Cadillac Records*. The music that Willie Dixon and his colleagues create eventually finds listeners beyond black communities, where it's popularized by effete British lads who thrill audiences worldwide with their watered-down versions. By then, the music is not so black. Or is it? Does it retain its indefinable essence in other settings?

Those are among the questions raised by "Nineteen Fifty-Five," Alice Walker's classic short story. Its protagonist, Gracie Mae Still, is a retired jook-joint singer who sells one of her tunes to a white talent manager and his Elvis-like protégé for one thousand dollars. Traynor, "with real dark white skin and a red pouting mouth," becomes a huge star with his note-for-note cover version of Gracie's composition. "If I'da closed my eyes, it could have been me," Gracie recalls. "He had followed every turning of my voice, side streets, avenues, red lights, train crossings and all. It give me a chill."

A year later, Traynor tells her he's earning forty thousand dollars a day from his recording. But he's uneasy, he admits, because "I don't have the faintest notion what that song means." As the years pass, Traynor, insecure and guilt-ridden, sends Gracie a multitude of presents, including a mink stole, a self-cleaning oven, a power tiller for her garden and, ultimately, a five-hundred-acre farm. Unlike his many admirers, Traynor understands that the performance that made him rich is but a pale imitation of the original. "They want what you got but they don't want you," he tells Gracie. "They want what I got only it ain't mine. That's what makes 'em so hungry for me when I sing. They getting the flavor of something but they ain't getting the thing itself."

In her homespun dialogue, the faux-sincerity of Gracie's visitors and the trail of twisted treaties between the unpretentious blueswoman and the music manager, Walker offers up a plausible and compelling thumbnail portrait of the American experience. Her Gracie comes off as a woman who could have rivaled Big Mama Thornton, the iconic blues belter from whom Elvis liberally borrowed. Instead, Gracie opted for something resembling domestic tranquility. As she tells it, she grew tired of "singing in first one little low-life jook joint after another, making ten dollars a night for myself if I was lucky, and sometimes bringin' home nothing but my life."

Revisiting Gracie Mae decades after Walker introduced her, I thought not of Big Mama Thornton but of Vera Hall. Born in Sumpter County, Alabama, in 1902, she lived a mostly obscure life as a domestic worker, although she was known throughout her community as a talented singer. Her noteworthy ability to remember gospel and blues songs she had heard little more than once eventually provided an invaluable resource to ethnomusicologists who set out during the 1930s to record black Southern music. On the recordings, Hall's voice sounds husky and clear at the same time; a hum runs through her vocals, and her singing conveys a lived-in quality that suggests heft and wisdom. In some tunes, like "Boll Weevil Holler" and "Wild Ox Moan," she adheres to her upper range, showing off a twang that nearly matches a strummed guitar string. These days she is best known for "Trouble So Hard," in which she shows off an abundance of that soulful ingredient that nonblack people often rely on to add accent to their music, like a blend of secret herbs and spices that makes chicken finger-licking good. Think Merry Clayton on "Gimme Shelter," Chaka Khan lending animation to Steve Winwood's "Higher Love," the countless gospel choirs blessing everything from Foreigner's "I Want to Know What Love Is" to Billy Joel's "The River of Dreams." In the video version of the latter, Joel cavorts stiffly like a low-rent Blues Brother, singing about his search for something "taken out of his soul." The all-black choir, garbed in church robes, helps him mourn "something somebody stole."

The scene makes me think of Amiri Baraka's poem "In the Tradition" in which he exposes the nation's cultural heritage as woefully deficient without the contributions of black people. "Where is your American music?" he taunts, declaring that "nigger music" might be all there is. Perhaps, he suggests, country and western music could save white America from "looking like saps before the world."

Merry Clayton and others, celebrated for their session

work, were paid for their contributions. In contrast, Hall's version of "Trouble So Hard" was plucked from the archives by a white techno musician named Moby, retitled "Natural Blues," and used to form the basis of a commercial hit in 2000. He also licensed it for use in an ad campaign for blue jeans. By then, Hall was long dead, and no descendants were contacted for permission or consultation.

Vera Hall didn't live to see her brilliance line other people's pockets, but Chuck Berry saw it unfold right before his eyes. In Darnell Martin's framing of the scene in *Cadillac Records*, Berry discovers the Beach Boys singing "Surfin' USA," a nearly note-for-note rip-off of his "Sweet Little Sixteen," just as police are coming to arrest him on morality charges. In real life, he sued the California band in 1963, winning the publishing rights and, three years later, formal songwriting credit. Like Berry, Willie Dixon knew how to take his complaints to court. In 1972, he sued Led Zeppelin over two songs on their second album, *II*. He won hefty settlements from the band, and later successfully sued Chess Records for back royalties.

As *Cadillac Records* tells it, Leonard Chess handed out keys to luxury cars to his musicians instead of their rightful compensation. The one exception in the film is Howlin' Wolf, who sticks with his battered truck and declines cash advances, refusing to "borrow against the store." Cadillacs, once the symbol of American aspiration, also function symbolically in "Nineteen Fifty-Five." One Christmas morning, Gracie Mae goes outside and discovers yet another token of Traynor's gratitude, a brand-new "gold-grilled white Cadillac." She enjoys the gift but never lets its shininess distract her from more practical concerns. The same can't be said for Muddy Waters, who allows the sight of a new car to make him forget—temporarily—Chess's mismanagement of his earnings. As Waters, Jeffrey Wright illustrates the mesmerizing power of the car when he wordlessly circles the first one Chess gives him, beaming in admiration. Not for nothing does Chuck Berry's 1973 Eldorado convertible sit on display in the Smithsonian's National Museum of African American History & Culture.

Cadillacs turn up, too, in *Dreamgirls*, a thinly veiled musical retelling of the Motown story. Label founder Curtis Taylor contends that the new sound rising from black urban communities could be made to seem as desirable as gleaming chrome and whitewall tires. It's almost as if he's read Jack Kerouac's *On the Road* in which the protagonist walks through a black neighborhood in Denver, "wishing I were a Negro, feeling that the best the white world had offered was not enough ecstasy for me, not enough life, joy, kicks, darkness, music, not enough night." Where beatniks and hipsters saw blackness as an aphrodisiac, Curtis sees a business opportunity. He sings, "If the big white man can make us think we need his Cadillac to make us feel as good as him, we can make him think he needs our music to make him feel as good as us." In an example of what we might call a mega-meta-mash-up, a black character makes this pronouncement about white characters in a fictional musical narrative inspired by real-life black people but written, composed, and directed by white people. Unlike Willie Dixon, Curtis Taylor doesn't possess the narrator's power to edit and shape the story. The *Dreamgirls* creative team gets it right, though, when their production shows Curtis's gritty, soulful paean to Cadillacs bleached and repackaged as a vanilla-scented parody of street-corner harmony.

Others' tendency to poach—and profit—from blackness is what makes its celebrants so watchful and suspicious. I am far less fretful, partly because my own creative practices borrow so freely from cultural traditions to which I enjoy no obvious connection. My influences and inept emulations are often painfully obvious to me, and in the event they are not so clear to observers, I try to give credit where it's due. Unlike that of Vera Hall or Walker's fictional heroine, my output is unlikely to command huge sums for anyone desperate enough to imitate me. Even so, I understand that to compare the transgressions (if you can call them that) of the marginalized to those of the imitative majority is to construct a false equivalency. More is at stake, and the record of theft, distortion, and dishonest revision is too real, too malignant and durable, to casually dismiss.

2

At the turn of the twentieth century, W. E. B. DuBois joined Frederick Douglass, Maria W. Stewart, and other pioneering black thinkers in declaring himself a coauthor of the collective American story. In *The Souls of Black Folk*, he claimed the Western canon as his birthright. It had been enriched, after all, via the plunder of black culture as well as black bodies. "I sit with Shakespeare, and he winces not," he contended. Some sixty years later, Ellison, while clinging tenaciously to blackness, also insisted on the right to keep company with storytellers of his own choosing, including Freud, Malraux, and Gertrude Stein. Like the bluesman Willie Dixon, both writers asserted the right of African Americans to relate the story of black creativity according to their own terms. At the same time, they pushed against the gates of the canon, the white, mostly male center of American culture. Its guardians borrowed freely from the wellspring of black creativity while keeping its originators outside the barriers. In such circumstances, borrowing often looks more like stealing.

Ellison was chafing against white critics like Irving Howe, who championed Richard Wright as the spiritual and intellectual godfather of "appropriate" African American fiction. In "Blueprint for Negro Writing," Wright had urged each black writer to create work that "would do no less than create values by which his race is to struggle, live and die." Ellison had little tolerance for such prescriptions, insisting instead that novels were "ritualistic and ceremonial at their core" and should "arise out of an impulse to celebrate human life." In some respects, this was an old dispute. Wright issued his blueprint in 1937, just nine years after Langston Hughes had staked a claim for his generation's creative independence in "The Negro Artist and the Racial Mountain." In "The World and the Jug," Ellison argued that white people couldn't tell black artists what to do; Hughes, in his "Racial Mountain" essay, had asserted that not even black people could tell black artists what to do. "We younger Negro artists who create now intend to express our individual dark-skinned selves without fear or shame," he memorably declared. "If white people are pleased we are glad. If they are not, it doesn't matter. We know we are beautiful. And ugly too. The tom-tom cries and the tom-tom laughs. If colored people are pleased, we are glad. If they are not, their displeasure doesn't matter either."

Both essays were volleys in the early modern phase of narrative combat, and both men were engaged in a fight over critical aspects of the black story, including who gets to tell it and what the rules are. In his memoir, *The Big Sea*, Hughes recalled his early days in Harlem as "a period when white writers wrote about Negroes more successfully (commercially speaking) than Negroes did about themselves." He also cited critics who condemned "certain Negro writers" who "ceased to write to amuse themselves and began to write to amuse and entertain white people." Although terms and phrases like "appropriation" and "selling out" were not yet in vogue, Hughes, Wright, and Ellison's salvos suggest that concerns about such issues seldom faded in black literary circles, even as the decades unfolded.

Frank Yerby, an African American writing during the same period, interests me because he maneuvered around those two land mines to claim his own narrow—and lucrative—patch of turf. He published his debut novel in 1946, the same year Muddy Waters plugged in his amp at the Chess brothers' studio. Ellison and James Baldwin had yet to publish their first titles, but Wright's career was already three books deep. "I was not at all influenced by him as a writer, except perhaps negatively," Yerby later recalled. "I liked, admired his earlier books; but if they influenced me at all, it was to confirm my growing suspicion that the race problem was not a theme for me." He was further convinced by the failure of his first manuscript, rejected by publishers looking either for racial stereotypes or the next Richard Wright. Frustrated, Yerby took an unusual step. Starting with *The Foxes of Harrow*, he wrote novels that focused primarily on white characters. Although never a critical darling, he attracted a willing—and white—audience among the masses. Over a forty-year period, he produced more than thirty novels and, astonishingly, sold more than sixty million copies worldwide. The

New York Times described him as "one of the most popular writers in the United States in the 1940's and 50's." His abundant sales to a primarily white readership enabled a comfortable life in France and Spain, where he died in 1992.

Although not quite bodice-rippers, many of Yerby's novels have more in common with Margaret Mitchell than with any of his African American contemporaries. Scoundrels challenge rascals to duels. Women compete for men's affection while weeping copiously. Some of them shed "great tears" that spill over "incredibly long lashes, gleaming like diamond drops in the candle flame"; others have eyes that "swam with tears that caught the light like jewels." Costumes and finery are minutely detailed. And there are sighs, lots of sighs. The wind sighs. Willows sigh. Women sigh, when they aren't weeping.

The Foxes of Harrow traces the adventures of Stephen Fox, an Irish gambler who lands in New Orleans in 1825, quickly amasses a fortune and a vast estate, and wins the hand of the most eligible belle in the Crescent City. While Fox and his family cavort and conspire in the foreground, people of the African diaspora populate the backdrop, with "brutes," "ragged blacks," mulattos, and quadroons occasionally emerging as plot devices or comic relief. Aside from the "light yellow" beauties, they are described in consistently unflattering terms. Black people are routinely debased not just in the dialogue of the white characters actively oppressing them but also in the omniscient narration, to such an extent that one may occasionally suspect that Yerby is a self-hating Negro.

The pivotal exception is Tante Caleen. First among Stephen Fox's "nearly fifteen hundred" enslaved human beings, she comes closest to what we might consider a fully realized black character. Her importance is hinted at during Yerby's well-written prologue in which she is the only figure among his sizable cast to be mentioned by name. Suspected of having voodoo powers, Caleen is a veteran trickster, cultivating whites' grudging respect while manipulating their fear and distrust of African spirituality. In possession of a seemingly boundless knowledge of herbs and elixirs, she is often called upon to heal white people after their doctors have failed to ease their suffering. Lest we grow too attached to Caleen, Yerby regularly reminds us that she is as physically unattractive as the other dark-skinned black people in the novel, with a face resembling "a grotesque death mask out of Africa" and "yellow, fanglike teeth" that gleam dully.

Out of many passages likely to dishearten African American readers, the most deflating one takes place when Caleen exploits a secret, intuitive method of communication among the enslaved to bring about a change of critical importance.

"I sing a song, me, out in the kitchen house," she explains. "Maîtresse hear me sing it a hundred time, but tonight I sing it different, just one sound different; hold one word a little too long, maybe. Cook, her hear me sing it. She hear that one word held too long. She go outside to empty water and she sing it too, her."

In this way, the song goes from mouth to mouth until Negroes "from every plantation in fifty miles" gather "in the black bayous when the moon is dark." But Caleen and the others don't employ their black girl magic in the pursuit of liberation. Instead, they direct their energy toward helping a lovelorn white woman regain her slaveholding husband's affection. The scene would be almost unbearable if Yerby hadn't already revealed that Caleen is the central figure in a family history of uprising and resistance.

Yerby lets us know that the face Caleen presents to her white oppressors is, as Paul Laurence Dunbar would put it, a mask that grins and lies. Her forbearance and apparent selflessness are part of an elaborate ruse conducted with an all-important goal in mind. "We can't win by fightin', us. They too strong," she advises her son. "We got to be clever like a swamp fox. . . . You learn. Learn to read and write and figger. But keep your mouth shut. Learn everything white man knows. . . . Someday freedom come."

When reading *Foxes* with Caleen's story uppermost in mind, I can easily imagine a different novel simmering in its depths: an epic saga in which African American characters love and struggle while Caleen leads readers through the labyrinthine complexities of blackness in nineteenth-century New Orleans. Despite Yerby's disavowals, I'm not entirely convinced that he wasn't indeed perpetrating a bit of narrative sleight of hand, that my alternate vision wasn't part of his grand design. Was he subverting a predictable tale of white pluck and ambition by planting a potentially explosive story of black resistance within it? Even if not, his novel certainly reflects the tensions surrounding culture and influence percolating at the time of its creation. And, while Yerby kept his distance from Wright's considerable shadow, his methods align comfortably with DuBois's insistence on inclusion and Hughes's assertion of independence. Yerby's parsing of American mythology, though overlong and uneven, argues that the story of the United States is not solely the province of whites. It belongs to anyone who dares to tell it.

In subsequent novels, Yerby continues to focus on ambitious, white Americans who rise to the height of society via fortitude, charm, and judicious coupling. In his fifth novel, *A Woman Called Fancy*, Fancy Williamson, like Stephen Fox before her, blows into town (in this case, Augusta, Georgia), with little to her name besides her wits and good looks. After having fled the South Carolina hills to escape an arranged marriage, she is determined to walk down the aisle arm in arm with a gentleman. On its most obvious level, the novel is about a difficult romance between the uncouth Fancy and Court Brantley, the least degenerate member of a genteel family fallen into disrepute. On another level, it's a story of class conflict among whites, with black characters playing a smaller part than they did in *Foxes*. The wealthy whites (landowners, mill operators, and turpentine merchants) exploit the poor whites mercilessly, only occasionally using black people as a buffer. One mill owner, the novel's most conscientious capitalist, observes, "What in hellfire would happen to those pine-barren crackers if they didn't have the blacks to look down on? They'd go crazy—or revolt; because even European serfs don't live any worse than they do. Having the Negro to feel superior to kind of makes it up to them."

Yerby's white characters converse often about black people's alleged inferiority and rationalize their abuse of them. In contrast, he gives his African American characters far less voice or agency than they demonstrated in *Foxes*. Although the main action in *Fancy* takes place from 1880 to 1894, the Negroes in Augusta seem to have fewer resources and exhibit less resistance than they did before the Southern Rebellion. Reconstruction has come and gone, returning black people to the clutches of their former enslavers. Convict leasing has again bound them to the land, but Court wants no part of it. "It *is* slavery," he tells Fancy. "Hell, it's worse. In slavery times, a good Negro was a valuable possession. You fed and clothed and petted him like a good horse. But who gives a damn what happens to these chain-gang niggers? Kill 'em off, work 'em, starve 'em, beat 'em to death. There're always more."

Court's attitude is representative of white characters' views in *Fancy*; when they condemn the exploitation of black people, they do so mostly from an economic perspective emphasizing profits and losses, not as a result of moral indignation or concern for the human rights of the Negroes in their midst. Such passages remind me that a black writer is behind the scenes, seizing and contradicting narratives that had been mostly used to promote the national fantasy of American exceptionalism.

As in *Foxes*, black people are suspected of possessing supernatural qualities. Unlike the magical Negroes of that book, these characters must work their enchantments without drums, rituals, or whispered incantations. The chief conjurer is a version of Tante Caleen, essentially repackaged here as Old Maud, an "old scarecrow, old as the hills, and black as original sin." On first meeting, Maud quickly intuits that Fancy is in love with Court Brantley but has not yet won his heart. "Listen to me, chile," she cautions. "Don't let him get too close beforehand—not even 'cause you loves him and he wants to—or maybe 'cause you wants to. Marry him, lil' Miss Fancygal! Make him stand up in front of the preacher man. Git him hooked legal—then give him hell!" As for Fancy's rival, whom Court may be visiting, she tells her to "go right in that house and pull him out—yank out some of that yaller hair whilest you's at it. Snatch her bald-headed—teach her some respect—go on, lil' Miss Fancygal, go fight for your man!"

Like Tante Caleen, Maud has extraordinary insight into the complexities of romance and the ways of white folk. But she possesses little of Caleen's dignity or self-possession, qualities rarely reflected in black characters in *Fancy*.

By the time Yerby turned to fiction, featuring a predominantly black cast, his best writing days were behind him. In *The Dahomean*, published in 1971, he gives free rein to his weakness for purple prose. He saddles an epic historical saga set in a West African kingdom with even more of the fluttery clichés found in his earlier novels. In Yerby's nineteenth-century Dahomey, young women have faces of "smoothly oval nightshade," "soft, velvety, night-black cheeks," and yes, "long, sweeping lashes." Nyasanu, his hero, is "a young lion with a heart more tender than a maid's." Scoundrels challenge rascals to duels. Women compete for men's affection while weeping copiously, and metaphors are driven home with mind-numbing repetitiveness. Agbale, Nyasanu's first wife, is described as a "tiny, exquisite, night-black girl." In case readers have failed to properly appreciate her loveliness, Yerby has Nyasanu remind us. He describes his bride as "my little black woman, more beautiful than the night." He goes on to explain, "Night is the time of love. And the color of night is black, which is the color of beauty." It's almost as if he was promised a cash bonus for each time he used "night" in the book.

In time, Nyasanu acquires additional wives, providing some of the most stomach-churning scenes in a novel with no shortage of such passages. After Nyasanu shows his wives that he is "capable of administering a husbandly beating when necessary," they grow to love and respect him even more. One wife says to him, "D'you know the first time in my life I've been truly happy? When you were beating me. When I realized that—that I meant so much to you that you'd kill me before letting me be another's easy woman. That you cared."

Nausea-inducing speeches of that sort—combined with clunky, circuitous prose—burden the novel so much that it inevitably sinks under its own weight. A plethora of foreign terms and exposition disguised as dialogue don't help Yerby's cause either, disrupting the narrative rhythm whenever he manages to establish it. In a "note to the reader" preceding the novel, he makes much of his "laborious" research. His toiling in the archives results too often in notebook dumping that dampens rather than sustains reader interest. Consequently, he strays far from his intended mission, which, after years of brazenly reimagining whiteness, is to set the record straight about Africa. He writes, "The purpose of *The Dahomean*, apart from the only legitimate purpose of any novel, entertaining the reader, is admittedly to correct so far as it is possible, the Anglo-Saxon reader's historical perspective."

Yerby's embrace of such a didactic strategy must have ultimately disappointed him. Ten years after *The Dahomean*, he would again insist that addressing racial issues in fiction was "an artistic dead end." In 1971, however, he may have been reentering the battle over the black narrative and reaching out to black readers, both of which he had abandoned long ago.

3

Or Yerby may have been reacting to writers like William Styron. Four years before *The Dahomean*, Styron had published *The Confessions of Nat Turner*. He had won acclaim in white literary circles for his debut novel *Lie Down in Darkness* but had attracted little comment beyond that hermetic, self-serving subculture. *Confessions*, his fourth book, earned him brief, sizzling infamy in the considerably smaller world of African American letters. It is an essentially plotless novel about one of the most notorious plots in American history, Nat Turner's bloody 1831 rebellion in Southampton County, Virginia. There is no suspense because we all know the story will end with Turner's capture and imminent execution. Perhaps desperate to seize and hold readers' attention, Styron settles for the easy option of lurid melodrama.

"I have allowed myself the utmost freedom of imagination in reconstructing events," he notes in his foreword, "yet I trust remaining within the bounds of what meager enlightenment history has left us about the institution of slavery. . . . Perhaps the reader will wish to draw a moral from this narrative, but it has been my intention to try to re-create a man and his era, and to produce a work that is less an 'historical novel' in conventional terms than a meditation on history."

Setting aside his ill-informed suggestion that the practice of human bondage in the United States has been meagerly documented, it is worth noting that Styron incorporates several relevant terms that we might call buzzwords: *narrative*, *imagination*, and *intention*. Of course one wants to allow Styron and other artists free rein in their works of imagination, although it is fair to wonder about the role of *research and field work* in creating paintings, books, etc., purportedly based on or inspired by the struggles of real people. Has the author ever interacted with black people in a genuine fashion— beyond the one or two he claims as "friends"? Reading

Confessions, it's hard to shake the suspicion that Styron is more familiar with the abject sufferers in *Uncle Tom's Cabin* than with living, breathing black human beings.

His intentions notwithstanding, it would be more accurate to describe his novel as a meditation on imagination, not history; he based it on the real-life Turner's "confession" as obtained by Thomas Gray. Styron concedes in his 1993 afterword that the slender pamphlet "from the first word . . . poses serious questions of veracity." This is an understatement, to say the least. Never has a confession of a crime, given privately by an African American while in legal custody, posed any other kind of question. Styron appears to offer a cursory nod to the tradition of doctored confessions here and there in his text. He has Thomas Gray say to Nat, for example, "This ain't supposed to represent your exact words as you said them to me. Naturally in a court confession there's got to be a kind of, uh, dignity of style." In Gray's unsolicited and unreliable editing of Turner's story, Styron provides a persuasive metaphor for narrative combat at its most insidious: a white man putting words in a black man's mouth.

Despite acknowledging his own doubts about Gray's report, Styron referred to it often during his defense against black critics who challenged the quality of his novel. In his attempt to use history to justify his appropriation of an iconic African American narrative, Styron returned repeatedly to a transcript that is likely more fancy than fact.

As for Styron's mission to re-create Turner, he has produced not a man but a cartoon. In his critique of the novel, African American author Lerone Bennett Jr. accused Styron of waging literary war on Turner's image, "substituting an impotent, cowardly, irresolute creature of his own imagination for the real black man who killed or ordered killed real white people for real historical reasons." Styron attributes Turner's motives to psychosexual obsessions with white women instead of a desire to set black people free and punish their enslavers. And, while we have no genuine knowledge of Turner's actual thoughts and conversations, the dialogue Styron burdens him with is nonetheless staggering to behold. A small but indicative sampling:

> It seemed rather that my black shit-eating people were surely like flies, God's mindless outcasts, lacking even that will to destroy by their own hand their unending anguish. . . .
>
> Yet I will say this, without which you cannot understand the central madness of nigger existence: beat a nigger, starve him leave him wallowing in his own shit, and he will be yours for life. Awe him by some unforeseen hint of philanthropy, tickle him with the idea of hope, and he will want to slice your throat. . . .
>
> I can see around me a score of faces popeyed with black nigger incredulity, jaws agape, delicious shudders of fright coursing through their bodies as they murmur soft *Amens*, nervously cracking their knuckles and making silent vows of eternal obedience.
>
> I feel a sense of my weakness, my smallness, my defenselessness, my niggerness invading me like a wind to the marrow of my bones.

Turner offers these reflections when he's not masturbating while dreaming of white women. During his weekly self-pleasuring sessions in a storage shed, "it was always a nameless white girl between whose legs I envisioned myself—a young girl with golden curls" with "her lips half open and whispering." Other sources of his fantasies do indeed have names. They include Miss Emmeline, for whom he "yearned with a kind of raw hunger," and Margaret Whitehead: "I could throw her down and spread her young white legs and stick myself in her until belly met belly and shoot inside her in warm milky spurts of desecration." Who talks like that? Probably not an enslaved African American in nineteenth-century Virginia. Nat longs to kill Margaret, "to snap that white, slender, throbbing young neck" as much as he'd like to do other things with her. Reading about Turner's tormented and volatile fascination, I half expected him to carve out Margaret's liver and have sex with it. As if anticipating his audience's concerns, he assures us that his craven lust is far from unique; it's a form of distorted passion that comes with the skin. "In later life," he tells us, "I learned that such an infatuation for a beautiful white mistress on the part of a black boy was not at all uncommon, despite the possibility of danger." Well, then, that explains it.

As for Styron's renderings of black women, calling them cartoons would be uncharitable—to cartoons. On those rare occasions when he bothers to mention them, they appear in Turner's memories as wanton playthings of easy virtue. The one black woman he fantasizes about is nothing like the quasivirginal white princesses that usually stir his loins. He describes the girl as "a plump doxy, every nigger boy's Saturday piece." Similarly, he speaks derisively of "the available and willing little black girls" who could be "taken" during "some quick stolen instant at the edge of a cornfield" or "lured behind a shed."

If there is a black woman or girl worthy of dignified treatment in all of Southampton County, Styron's Turner has never seen her.

Most appalling of all is Turner's mother, whom he witnesses being transported to heights of glorious ecstasy as a white rapist brutally assaults her on a kitchen table. The scene combines absurdity and horror and leaves behind a lingering distaste. At the book's end, we are left to wonder if Styron can—or even desires to—compose a black female character of texture and dimension.

Turner's frenzied preoccupation with white women often swells to such proportions that it drowns out all other thoughts, including any notion of escape or freedom. The prospect of manumission renders him utterly perplexed. "*A free man*," he reflects. "Never in a nigger boy's head was there such wild sudden confusion." Styron piles on the injuries and insults throughout, upping the yuck factor as he proceeds. In one scenario, a white sadist named Nathaniel Francis forces a dimwitted enslaved man to have sex with a dog. In another, he makes two slaves engage in brutal hand-to-hand combat. Each of these acts takes place in front of an audience. Forced bestiality, dominance, and submission—the scenes unfold like pages from an S&M novel in which the masochists have no safe words. It's not hard to imagine Styron drooling over his sheets of yellow legal paper as he feverishly scribbled, shuddering from every burst of emotion that comes from writing *nigger* more than 240 times.

Because Styron never claimed to be attempting satire, we are obliged to take seriously the idea that he took his novel seriously. In the accidental farce that emerges, the fictional Turner often speaks as if he expects that no black person will ever get to read his confession. The same is true of his creator, who seems to have written the novel solely with a white audience in mind and hadn't genuinely considered that black people would read it. James Baldwin, Styron fondly recalls in his foreword, encouraged him to overcome his hesitations and "take on the persona of Nat Turner and write as if from within this black man's skin." To ward off the hailstorm of denunciation from African Americans that descended soon after the novel's publication, Styron resorted to a variation on a classic defense, declaring, in essence, "Some of my best friends are Baldwin." For his part, Baldwin remained steadfast, standing by Styron with mostly nondescript pronouncements such as "No one can tell a writer what he should write" (true) and "Styron is probing something very dangerous, deep and painful in the national psyche" (also true).

The eminent historian John Hope Franklin endorsed the novel, but other black admirers were hard to find. In an afterword to the 1993 edition, Styron mentions the warm reception he received at a historically black college, but I wonder if any members of the faculty or administration had actually peered between the book's covers. If they had, they probably noted some of the ways in which the novel could be seen as awkwardly conversant with works by black novelists such as Wright and essayists like Baldwin.

For instance, in Styron's *Confessions*, an enslaved man named Hark is persecuted after stumbling upon two white boys engaged in mutual masturbation, causing Nat to ponder what he considered an uncorrectable condition: "White people really see nothing of a Negro in his private activity, while a Negro, who must walk miles out of his path to avoid seeing everything white people do, has often to suffer for even the most guileless part of his ubiquitous presence by being called a spy and a snooping black scoundrel." The passage recalls Wright's recollections in *Black Boy* of working as a bellboy in a Southern hotel:

I grew used to seeing the white prostitutes naked upon their beds, sitting nude about their rooms, and I learned new modes of behavior, new rules in how to live the Jim Crow life. It was presumed that we black boys took their nakedness for granted, that it startled us no more than a blue vase or a red rug. Our presence awoke in them no sense of shame whatever, for we blacks were not considered human anyway. If they were alone, I would steal sidelong glances at them. But if they were receiving men, not a flicker of my eyelids would show.

Another Styron passage seems influenced by this scene in *Black Boy* at the optical lens shop where Wright had been hired:

But one day Reynolds called me to his machine.

"Richard, how long is your thing?" he asked me.

"What thing?" I asked.

"You know what I mean," he said. "The thing the bull uses on the cow."

I turned away from him; I had heard that whites regarded Negroes as animals in sex matters and his words made me angry.

"I heard that a nigger can stick his prick in the ground and spin around on it like a top," he said, chuckling. "I'd like to see you do that. I'd give you a dime, if you did it."

In a similar scene in *Confessions*, twenty-year-old Nat is being transported to his new home by Reverend Eppes, the man to whose keeping he has been entrusted.

> "Tell me something, boy," he said finally, the reedy voice suddenly strained, hesitant yet fraught with some terrible decision. "I hear tell a nigger boy's got an unusual big pecker on him. That right, boy?"
>
> When Nat doesn't reply, Reverend Eppes persists. "You know what I hear tell, boy? I hear tell your average nigger boy's got a member on him inch or so longer'n ordinary. That right, boy?"

Styron's practice of echo and revision recalls Langston Hughes's observations about white writers quoted earlier in this essay, along with his 1940 poem, "Note on Commercial Theatre." In it, a black blues artist complains that whites have "mixed" and "fixed" his creations "so they don't sound like me." Not much later, Styron appears to challenge an oft-quoted observation of his friend Baldwin. Four years earlier, the fiery prophet had famously declared in *Time* magazine, "To be black and conscious in America is to be in a constant state of rage." Styron's Turner offers a far more reassuring take on the same subject. "An exquisitely sharpened hatred for the white man is of course an emotion not difficult for Negroes to harbor," he says. "Yet if truth be known, this hatred does not abound in every Negro's soul; it relies upon too many mysterious and hidden patterns of life and chance to flourish luxuriantly everywhere." Granted, hate and rage are not necessarily the same thing. Still, Styron's Turner seems determined to minimize the possibility of black resentment.

Like Wright and Baldwin, Styron convincingly

exposes white neuroses and hypocrisies. The historical record assisted all three writers in this regard (including the well-documented obsession with black sexuality and the tendency of lynch mobs to practice genital mutilation). In contrast, the behavior of the fictional Turner and his fellow captives seems to have sprung entirely from Styron's imagination, with little correspondence to be found in actual histories of life under enslavement.

Styron's "liberties" prompted several black thinkers to join John Henrik Clarke in compiling an essay collection, *William Styron's Nat Turner: Ten Black Writers Respond.* It could just have easily been called *Why Styron Sucks.* Most of the essayists remark on the fictional Turner's inexplicable obsession with white women, while the absence of black women characters who aren't whores almost completely escapes comment. Clarke and company frequently question Styron's motives, knowledge of African American culture, and command of history. An element of recoil animates all the essays, with many of them exuding an almost palpable sense of disgust. This is understandable: Reading the novel the first time, I felt as if I was peeking at a blackface party through a frat-house window. Reading it again produced the same sensation.

A visceral response to Styron's manipulations might induce some readers to concentrate on his objective and state of mind while overlooking important questions of craft. And craft, inevitably, is where he falls short. The undisciplined fecundity of his prose buries Turner's voice and personality under obscuring layers of verbiage. Styron seldom settles for one or two modifiers when a half dozen will do. The flat, rhythmless sentences often seem out of place in an exploration of cultural space where rhythm—of

speech, song, and gesture—was a vital resource for enslaved captives trying to get through the day. This lack
strains credulity even when one is willing to suspend
disbelief to engage the requirements of a fictional narrative. As Vincent Harding points out in his essay, "You've
Taken My Nat and Gone," "The religious music of Afro-
Americans never enters as a major structural element of
the novel as one would expect if such a work had been
done by an Ellison, a Baldwin, or a Wright." Styron,
who earned more than a million dollars from the
novel, became that rare usurper of black cultural history who left music relatively untouched, ignoring the
art form traditionally most vulnerable to poaching for
profit.

Unsurprisingly, white reviewers reacted quite differ-
ently to *The Confessions of Nat Turner*. They praised the
book in the *Nation*, the *New York Review of Books*, the
Wall Street Journal, *Commentary*, the *New York Times*,
Vogue, *Newsweek*, *Partisan Review*, and *Dissent*, among
others. Could so many critics have gotten it wrong? Apparently. Mike Thelwell, writing in *Ten Black Writers Respond*, noted, "If this book is important, it is so not
because it tells much about Negro experience during slavery but because of the manner in which it demonstrates
the persistence of white southern myths, racial stereotypes, and literary clichés even in the best intentioned
and most enlightened minds. Their largely uncritical acceptance in literary circles shows us how far we still have
to go."

Like the clueless crowds who adore Alice Walker's
hapless antihero in "Nineteen Fifty-Five," Styron's boosters
exalted a pale approximation of a story of black struggle.
They got neither the flavor nor the thing itself.

4

Appropriation was once associated with unprincipled borrowing from a minority population's art or culture, or shameless imitations that pretended to be the original. Nowadays, in discussions among African Americans, it seems to refer more often to a borrowing of black experience (and most often, black pain) in which the very act of borrowing, with or without attribution, is a form of inexcusable disrespect. Making money from culture acquired under questionable circumstances just adds insult to injury, affirming the oft-expressed complaint that black culture matters but black lives don't. Within that context, Nat Turner's uprising remains a significant source of pride and sadness among African Americans; pride in his courage and his commitment to secure liberation by any means necessary, and sadness stemming from the hundreds of black people that suffered abuse and violent death as a result of his actions. Long before William Styron shared his cursory impressions of Turner's rebellion with his fawning readership, Turner had achieved and maintained folk hero status among black people. He was, in the words of African American critic Albert Murray, "a magnificent forefather enshrined in the National Pantheon beside the greatest heroes of the Republic."

In the mid-twentieth century, Emmett Till attained a similarly mythical status. Jesus, they say, rose after three days. Emmett did too. After his abductors tortured and killed him, they tied a seventy-pound cotton gin fan around what was left of his neck. Wanting no one to know how much he'd suffered for the sins of his nation, they tossed his remains into the Tallahatchie River. No doubt his were not the only bones there. Find any ground where black people toiled in the Jim Crow South, any body of water that bore witness to their labors, sift the soil, dredge the depths, and you are bound to find some bones. Consecrate those bones, the poet Henry Dumas had urged. Dumas, black bard, son of the rural South, envisioned the bones—"big bones and little bones, parts of bones, chips, tid-bits, skulls, fingers and everything"—hauled up and handled like "babies or somethin' precious."

But most of those bones are stuck in the earth, working their way deeper into time. Not Emmett's. They still had flesh upon them and they rose to the surface, where things done in the dark are brought to light.

Mamie Till, Emmett's mother, would not allow a closed casket after the body was brought to the North. What's more, she permitted a photographer from *Jet* magazine to photograph the corpse. Anyone who's seen the resulting image is likely to remember it. It may not hit you at first. You might think you're looking at a geological survey, a star-charred chunk of meteor, or a satellite image of a distant planet. But then you notice a hint of nostrils, a trace of lips perched illogically atop the ruin, or you see a photograph of Emmett helpfully juxtaposed, see him in the robust beauty of youth, the softness still apparent on the face of the boy becoming a man. Adulthood was right around the corner but Emmett never got there. Mamie Till wanted us to know why he didn't.

When she arranged his battered remains in an open casket, more than fifty thousand black Chicagoans lined up to view the body. Today, Till's casket, exhumed in 2004 when a grand jury reopened his case, sits on display in the

Smithsonian's Museum of African American History and Culture.

Five floors above the casket, *Behold Thy Son* hangs on a wall. David Driskell's oil painting, rendered in subtle variations of copper and bronze, is a poignant portrait of Mamie Till holding the body of her only son, Emmett. At forty inches by thirty inches, it's roughly the dimensions of a bath towel. Many critics have noted the religious overtones of the painting, including its title (taken from the Bible, John 19:26), its suggestion of stained glass, and the robed mother supporting Till's body. The young man's arms are fully extended, echoing Christ splayed on the cross. Ambiguity pervades the scene: The woman could be helping the youth to stand or preparing his body for burial. His face, though distorted, doesn't closely resemble Till's, and the body's wounds are muted and indistinct. We know the figure is Till because Driskell has suggested as much; otherwise, it could be anyone from Jesus to an anonymous mother's son. The vagueness is meant to connect Till's death to notions of universal loss and suffering. (While shared trauma simmers at the core of much African American art, it would be a mistake to overestimate its centrality. It's important to note that collective pain coexists in the same space with many other elements, including joy, music, and sheer indomitability.)

Till's desecrated body washed up in the Tallahatchie River on August 31, 1955. Weeks later, Driskell and his family moved south so he could take a teaching job at Talladega College. By then, details of the young boy's murder had reached black communities across the country. The wounds were still fresh when the artist put brush to canvas. (In addition to the painting, Driskell produced two small sketches, *Behold Thy Son I* and *Behold Thy Son II*, which placed the Till figure in an open casket.) "This crime awakened in most African Americans a sense of rage that helped prepare us for the revolutionary journey we would eventually take," he has said. Part of that journey took place in jazz, experimental theater, and visual arts, where Driskell's painting played a seminal role. Although he was "well aware of the power of social commentary art and its use to stir the consciousness of a people," he quickly moved away from it in his painting. Because of *Behold Thy Son*, he said, "I kind of got it out of my system." While Driskell's efforts at issue-oriented art were ending, those of others were about to begin. It's not difficult to connect Driskell's work to the politically conscious artist collectives that followed in the next decade, including the Spiral Group in New York and AfriCobra in Chicago.

Driskell, born in 1931, would go on to become one of the most prominent painters, curators, and art scholars in the United States. He completed *Behold Thy Son* one year after Till's murder—and twenty years before painter Dana Schutz was born.

In 2017, three of Schutz's canvases were chosen for the Whitney Biennial. One of them, a fifty-three-by-thirty-nine-inch oil painting called *Open Casket*, uses the famous photograph of Till's body lying in state as a point of departure. The formal wear and the swollen dimensions of the head quickly orient those viewers who have seen the image. A streak of red, reminiscent of blood, runs parallel to the shirt's placket, which is punctuated by buttons that may remind some observers of bullet holes. The head is less grotesque than barely recognizable as such, its misshapen surfaces conveyed by broad brushstrokes and thick layers of brown paint. Unlike Driskell's painting, the finality of

Till's life on Earth is emphasized via the decay of flesh; Schutz provides viewers no hint of solace through quasi-religious suggestions of resurrection, redemption, or the protective vision of an unseen god. She conceived of the painting as "evidence of something that really happened," she explained to a reporter. "I wasn't alive then, and it wasn't taught in our history classes." Like Styron before her, she perceived a blank space in the historical narrative and used her imagination with the intention of filling it. Also like Styron, she stumbled into a firestorm of outrage and recrimination.

During the public opening of the Biennial on March 17, 2017, an African American artist named Parker Bright stood directly in front of *Open Casket*. Wearing a shirt with "Black Death Spectacle" written on the back, he remained between viewers and the painting for several hours. Bright's stance provided a hint of the furor to come; without saying a word, he had performed a bodacious public declaration, somewhat like yanking the mic from Taylor Swift at an award show. His position reminded me of similar, less dramatic debates that have frequently unfolded on social media. The desire to avoid seeing trauma has often played out in gripping Facebook threads in which black users have argued eloquently against the posting of video recordings of police shootings. Doing so compounds the horror, they contend, and it also provides lurid entertainment for white users titillated by the sight of broken blackness. The countless historical postcards of white men, women, and children grinning next to a pulverized, burned, and mutilated dark body prove that the latter is a real possibility. Even so, and despite the eloquence and passion of such arguments, I've never been persuaded to abide by them. I don't begrudge others the right to disregard disturbing images, but I always want to see for myself, even at the risk of providing free diversion for gazers with sordid motives. The opportunity to witness fuels my awareness of my own precarious citizenship, informs my understanding of our police state and, at critical times, has strengthened my willingness to resist. I won't insist that you look; neither should you demand that I don't. The same applies to paintings. Bright appeared to be interfering not only with "the white gaze" but also all gazes. Suppose I had tapped him on the shoulder and said, "Excuse me, brother." Would he have stepped aside?

Hannah Black, another black artist, increased the heat via a Facebook posting to the Biennial's curators. Among several salient observations about white supremacy, institutional racism, and antiblack violence, she called for the removal and destruction of *Open Casket*. She argued, "It is not acceptable for a white person to transmute Black suffering into profit and fun." Schutz's paintings don't typically depict black people and they were selling from $90,000 to $400,000 each before she was chosen for the Whitney Biennial. What's more, she has committed to never offering *Open Casket* for sale. In some cases, white artists have indeed appropriated black subjects for profit and increased fame, but it is difficult to make that argument here. According to Black, the sight of antiblack violence has seldom been "sufficient to move the white gaze from its habitual cold calculation."

"Seldom" isn't the same as "never"; occasionally exposure to injustice and brutality inspires an Abel Meeropol to compose "Strange Fruit" or motivates a Violet Liuzzo to leave her home and privilege behind to head down South and make the ultimate sacrifice. We should allow for that possibility, however slim it might be. The prospect of artists censoring other artists is more nauseating than having to suffer the output of creators whose reach exceeds their grasp. I would no sooner demand that Schutz destroy her canvas than I'd call for Lil Wayne to set fire to his recordings after spitting such egregious rhymes as "beat that pussy up like Emmett Till." Artists need the space to fail as much as they need the raw materials from which they fashion their work. And, although I'm more drawn to Driskell's interpretation of the Till tragedy, I hardly consider Schutz's version a failure.

I don't think Driskell's painting is aesthetically superior to Schutz's; to my eyes, they both are well done. Nor do I prefer Driskell's painting because he's black. It appeals to me because it encourages me to contemplate African Americans' creative darkening of Judeo-Christian theology. I'm not referring to the early years of our captivity when Moses and Jesus were forced upon us but to the years that have followed, during which many of us continue to embrace a God-story that wasn't ours to begin with. I'm not suggesting that our adoption is appropriation because it's absent any power dynamics implicit in that process. I am suggesting that it is a form of voluntary assimilation; the political utility of endorsing the Jesus story is often apparent to me. I'm interested in ways that artists like Driskell subvert that story by making it explicitly black, by canonizing marginalized and brutally oppressed black citizens like Till and Turner. Like the historic Afro-Caribbean practice of converting Catholic saints into neo-African deities, paintings such as *Behold Thy Son* can equip black viewers with the psychic armor they need to withstand the challenges of the predatory, unyielding West.

Driskell's painting leads me down corridors of intellectual inquiry that invariably challenge and surprise me.

Much of my response to the work is what I'm projecting onto it from my own background and thought process, a kind of projection that's beyond the artist's control. It's a way in which the art speaks—eloquently—for itself. That said, I am genuinely moved by Schutz's painting, and no less so because she is white. It simply appeals to me for different reasons than Driskell's does.

I believe it's possible to defend Schutz's project without underestimating the larger problem of institutional racism that keeps artists of color out of major museums and exhibitions. I share the anguish of many art lovers who despair that the conversation about Schutz seldom expanded to include the work of black women painters who've also responded to Till in their work. Lisa Whittington is among these, as is Melodye Benson Rosales, whose *The End of Innocence* is probably my favorite work in this category. Still, the argument for inclusion is more persuasive when one points to mediocre artists granted a spotlight that their work doesn't merit. (This is also a problem in publishing, where catalogs and bookstore shelves are crammed with white-authored work of questionable quality.) The problem with sweeping generalizations is they risk excluding art and artists who should be inside, not out. Few critics seem to be saying that Schutz's work is not good enough to be shown, which is a quite different argument from saying that her work is not appropriate.

5

Parallel Time, a memoir by Brent Staples, begins with a brilliant, chilling description of an autopsy photograph taken on February 13, 1984. Staples starts at the head ("squarish and overlarge") and proceeds to the feet, each of which has a second toe that "curls softly in an extended arc and rises above the others." In between, he describes the body's injuries resulting from being shot six times with a large-caliber handgun. Staples doesn't flinch, noting the enormous surgical wound that "runs the length of the abdomen, from the sternum all the way to the pubic mound," resembling "a mouth whose lips are pouting and bloody." The strength of his language notwithstanding, Staples's narrative gathers considerable power when he moves from the clinical to the visceral.

"His feelings are mine as well," he writes of the dead black man on the slab. "Cold: the sensation moves from my eyes to my shoulder blades to my bare ass as I feel him naked on the steel. I envision the reflex that would run through his body, hear the sharp breath he would draw when the steel met his skin. Below the familiar feet a drain awaits the blood that will flow from this autopsy."

The feet are familiar to Staples because they belonged to his younger brother. He goes on to mention the "terse narrative summary" of the coroner's report:

SKULL: Intact.
VERTEBRAE: Intact.
RIBS: Intact.
PELVIS: There is a chip fracture of the left pubic ramus, and there is also fracturing of the right pubic ramus. There is extensive fracturing of the left femur, and there is a through-and-through bullet wound of the right femur just below the hip joint.

The author effectively counters the report's sterile account with gut reactions and personal memories that offer a glimpse of Blake Melvin Staples as he lived and breathed. He reminds us that official documents can seldom convey the full humanity of a person and may even undermine it. What's more, Brent Staples demonstrates that scenes of black heartbreak can be turned into moments of reflection and illumination if handled with care. The risk of getting it wrong, a significant danger, even when the creative artist is African American, increases exponentially when the artist is not.

Across disciplines and centuries, black creators have shared a concern for what they regard as whites' mishandling of—and preoccupation with—black tragedy. As commonly perceived, this unseemly obsession usually takes one of two forms. In the first, white audiences derive perverse pleasure from black misery. The novelist Chester Himes identified this kind of racially inflected trauma porn before there was a name for it. In his 1972 memoir, *The Quality of Hurt*, he wrote, "I have never heard the phrase 'It's a beautiful book' applied to a book written by a black writer unless the black characters have suffered horribly. I have heard scores of white people say of Richard Wright's books *Native Son* and *Black Boy* that they were 'beautiful books.' Of course this does not mean the same thing to me as it does to these white people. The suffering of others does not fill me with any spiritual satisfaction. Nor do I revel in the anguish of my fellow human beings. I am not uplifted by other people's degradation."

In the second instance, white artists ruthlessly pillage the African American experience in search of fodder for their creations. This was one of the many nerves Hannah Black struck in her condemnation of *Open Casket*. Artists who aren't black, she argued, should "stop treating Black pain as raw material." A year before Dana Schutz was charged with doing exactly that, a white conceptual poet named Kenneth Goldsmith floundered into a similar quagmire. On March 13, 2015, he stepped before an audience at Brown University and read a poem called "The Body of Michael Brown."

Brown's killing at the hands of a policeman named Darren Wilson on August 9, 2014, remains a source of great agony in African American communities across the country. For many of us, it's hard to hear his name without recalling his body lying on the ground for more than four hours, the police preventing his mother from going to him, the killer's subsequent explanation that Brown "looked like a demon." Like Emmett Till before him, Brown has become an unwitting martyr in the endless struggle against antiblack violence. As a result, any artistic response to his death that seems callous or unthinking risks aggravating injuries that aren't remotely close to healing.

With a blown-up image of Brown's graduation photograph onscreen behind him, Goldsmith read for thirty minutes from the young man's autopsy report. About seventy-five people were present at the reading, and only a handful of them wrote about it afterward. Goldsmith asked the university to withhold the video recording of his performance from public view, so most of us know more about the controversy that followed than we do about the event itself. As news of Goldsmith's presentation spread, he quickly drew fire from the literary community and especially writers of color. Roxane Gay called his performance "tacky." The Mongrel Coalition against Gringpo, an anonymous collective of writers of color, accused Goldsmith of failing to "differentiate between White Supremacy and Poetry."

In an article about the dustup, the *New Yorker* helpfully compared the poet's stunt to *Fidget*, a previous work by Goldsmith in which he attempts to document every movement of his body from waking up at 10:00 a.m. to returning to sleep at 11:00 p.m. A good alternative title could be *Way Too Much Time on My Hands*. A typical passage reads like this: "Forefinger moves to nostril. Enters. Tip of finger probes ridge inside nostril. Shape of left nostril conforms to shape of finger. Shape of finger conforms to shape of left nostril." Beats working, I suppose.

According to critic Marjorie Perloff, who has championed Goldsmith's work, *Fidget* is "not literary invention but *poésie verité*, a documentary record of how it actually is when a person wakes up on a given morning." In a letter to Perloff, Goldsmith explained it this way: "Every move was an observation of *a* body in a space, not *my* body in a space. There was to be no editorializing, no psychology, no emotion—just a body detached from a mind." In that same letter, he wrote, "I was alone all day in my apartment and didn't answer the phone, go on errands, etc. I just observed my body and spoke."

As a result, I can't help seeing the figure being observed in *Fidget* not just as *a* body but a *white* one, and I'm tempted to consider the two projects not as companion pieces but studies in dramatic contrast: On one side, a live white body moving through space according to its own impulses; on the other, a dark, inert body, fatally punished for daring to move through space *as if* it were white (i.e., walking in the middle of the street). In his defense of his Michael Brown piece, Goldsmith declined to connect it to *Fidget*. Instead, he placed it "in the tradition" of his book *Seven American Deaths and Disasters*. In the book he transcribes and edits news broadcasts from fateful events in recent US history, including the assassination of John F. Kennedy and the explosion of the space shuttle *Challenger*. It *is* closer to "The Body of Michael Brown" in that both are revised texts made of words Goldsmith did not compose himself. He says that this method of "uncreative writing" enables him "to tell the truth in the strongest and clearest way possible."

Some of the most pointed criticisms of Goldsmith challenged his use of the autopsy report as the basis of a literary exploration. That was the one aspect of his project that I found intriguing, since such a document presents a challenge not only because it confronts readers with their own mortality but also, in this case, because of the pain that still surrounds Brown's death. Rereading the medical examiner's words almost four years after their initial release, I felt as nauseous as when I first read them. When filtered through the sensibilities of a gifted writer, an autopsy can be used to "wring the marvelous from the terrible," as Ellison would have it. The opening of Brent Staples's memoir is one example. Another is Sapphire's "Found Poem," from her *American Dreams* collection. It switches dexterously from the abrupt matter-of-factness of the coroner's language into a skillful use of repetition that dramatizes the violent consequences of a body beaten to death:

> *his shoulder shoulder shoulder blades*
> *have similar similar similar cuts*
> *where his attackers came down*
> *on his back*

Still another is Martín Espada's "How We Could Have Lived or Died This Way." The poet converts the bureaucratic prose of coroners' reports into weaponized words accompanying the police shootings that leave unarmed black bodies sprawled on city streets:

> *I see the coroner nodding, the words he types in his*
> *   report burrowing*
> *into the skin like more bullets. I see the government*
> *   investigations stacking,*
> *words buzzing on the page, then suffocated as bees*
> *   suffocate in a jar. I see*
> *the next Black man, fleeing as the fugitive slave once*
> *   fled the slave-catcher,*
> *shot in the back for a broken tail light. I see the cop*
> *   handcuff the corpse.*

If reports of Goldsmith's Brown University reading are accurate, his attempt at offering a poetic take on the autopsy report wasn't wrong in itself; the error was his failure to transform it from a record of raw tragedy into poetry that informs and disturbs. If one dares to insert oneself into the ongoing narrative of white supremacy and police brutality, one needs to come prepared. Whether he possessed the necessary skill, knowledge, and imagination to enter the fray remains an open question.

But we are left to speculate. Goldsmith pulled the plug on his Michael Brown poem, and the university sealed any evidence that the poet had been there at all.

He had taken the body and gone.

I'm so tired of waiting,
Aren't you,
For the world to become good
And beautiful and kind?
—Langston Hughes, "Tired"

OF LOVE AND STRUGGLE
THE LIMITS OF RESPECTABILITY

When Michelle Obama spoke at the Democratic convention in Los Angeles on July 25, 2016, she delivered an emphatic endorsement of the party's candidate for president, Hillary Clinton. But the words she said before mentioning Clinton attracted the most attention. She referred movingly to the challenges she confronted while raising her daughters in an often hostile political climate. "How we urge them to ignore those who question their father's citizenship or faith," she said. "How we insist that the hateful language that they hear from public figures on TV does not represent the true spirit of this country. How we explain that when someone is cruel or acts like a bully, you don't stoop to their level. No, our motto is, when they go low, we go high."

After eight years as First Lady, she had rightly acquired a reputation as a persuasive speaker. Much like her husband, she combines charm and good looks with a penetrating intellect. Righteous and fervent, her convention speech echoed Martin Luther King Jr.'s prayer during a 1957 oration: "God grant that right here in America and all over this world, we will choose the high way; a way in which men will live together as brothers. A way in which the nations of the world will beat their swords into plowshares, and their spears into pruning hooks."

As is the case with any black citizen who evokes the noble American spirit and suggests compassion in the face of hatred, she was praised for her eloquence and restraint. It was the kind of address, after all, that makes white moderates roar with delight and black believers fan themselves and shout "Amen!" Her advice to her daughters was indeed suitable for children navigating the school yard, if not as applicable for Democrats and independents battling a rising tide of Republican rancor and rebranded racism fueled by Trump's successful run for president. I understand that right-wing lies, insults, and smears, desperate and clueless as they are, are often unworthy of a dignified response; deigning to reply may confer more significance than ad-hoc racialisms deserve. There is tempting convenience in offering a dismissive *tsk-tsk* instead of dirtying one's hands via direct engagement. Clearly, Michelle Obama's response to her haters reflects those considerations. What interests me more is the speech's connection to the African American tradition of patient, refined dissent. As such, it both embodied and extended the stubborn shelf life of respectability politics, the approach that King advocated and that many (but not all) veterans of the civil rights struggle heartily endorsed. The philosophy wistfully suggests that turning a cheek and presenting clean teeth and fingernails will shame or otherwise persuade our oppressors to hold their fire.

The adherence to decorum as a defense against vitriol reminds me of attempts to cast every unarmed victim of police violence as an honor student, choirboy, Eagle Scout, and Red Cross volunteer. I'm aware that such efforts are partly in response to mainstream media's mostly uncritical digestion of police officers' deceptions. News organizations circulate law enforcement officials' questionable incident reports and suggestive photographs that criminalize and otherwise destroy the reputations of those whose bodies they've already desecrated. And, because many white people historically have tended to judge all black people on the behavior of an individual black person, the more respectable the deceased is, the better. (It's the reason why most African Americans, when learning of a criminal's rampage, say to themselves, "Please don't let him be black!") A black killer is a thug and a menace, whereas a white one is merely "troubled" or needs treatment that he deserved but never received. I get all that. It's a related sentiment I'm thinking of, the idea that an "honorable" black life, principled in word and deed, is somehow more valuable than a less virtuous one.

According to such fanciful thinking, our scrubbed, schooled, and obviously harmless presence will suggest to the millions of antiblack racists in our country, "If only you could see that I am good. Perhaps then you wouldn't want me dead." Or, when addressing the most passive of our self-described progressive allies, "If only you could truly believe that I am good. Perhaps then you wouldn't stand by in mock #outrage while a police officer shoots me dead." Miraculously, these epiphanies will take place in a Moral Cinematic Universe in which it has long been held that "the only good nigger is a dead one." (The Southern Poverty Law Center reports that *goodified* is racist slang for a murdered black person.) White moderates sometimes become smitten with a similar notion: the possibility that their racist counterparts simply haven't met the right black person, someone who could impress them as attractive, competent, and nonthreatening at the same time. Senator Harry Reid notably imagined that Barack Obama, "light-skinned with no Negro dialect," could be that person.

Years later, many black people sustained the same fantasy. To counter offensive racist caricatures, they took to posting Facebook images of the Obama family: articulate, moisturized, and scandal free. But instead of persuading racists to discover the error of their ways, the Obamas' luster merely inflamed their jealousy. Racist online comments protesting their White House occupancy led me to recall a scene from John Singleton's woefully underappreciated 1997 film *Rosewood*. Speaking about a character played by Don Cheadle, one member of a lynch mob says to another: "You know, he's got a piano. A nigger with a goddamn piano. I been working all my life. I ain't got a piano. That nigger's got one and I don't. Now, how does that look?"

It remains a profound and perhaps interminable paradox that African Americans are constantly striving to prove themselves worthy of citizenship in a country that has not proved itself ready for democracy. I'm intrigued and mystified by the enduring popularity of moral appeals and dutiful citizenship in black communities, especially while the movement for black lives has worked so hard to consign the politics of respectability to the dustbin of outdated ideas. The sight of prayerful Negroes in church clothes kneeling before bloodthirsty troopers with snarling dogs has undoubtedly awakened sympathy in some previously hardened racists. However, little evidence suggests that spit-shined activism has ever swayed a crucial majority of white Americans. Our struggle requires a multifaceted approach combining skillful diplomacy, daring gambits, *and* methodical endurance. Consequently, it seems that going high is an unfit response, to say, rapacious private prisons, heartless Republican congressional policy, and the sixty-three million Americans who voted for a racist demagogue. Instead of going high, we should be going everywhere.

> *Justice don't mean nothin' to a*
> *hateful heart!*
> . . . .
> *We needed a way around the hateful hearts of*
> *America.*
> —JUNE JORDAN, "JIM CROW: THE SEQUEL"

To overcome their oppressors, an embattled population needs superior numbers, superior weapons, or superior tactics. Our ancestors in America, having none of those, resorted to trying to make the battleground a moral one. Barack Obama paid homage to that tradition in a May 2017 speech given in defense of the Affordable Care Act. "I have said before that I believe what Dr. King said— that the arc of the moral universe bends, but it bends towards justice," he told the crowd. "I have also said that it does not bend on its own, but it bends because we bend it, and we put our hand on the arc and we move it in the direction of justice and freedom and equality and kindness and generosity. It does not happen on its own."

I seldom think in terms of good and evil. I rely on a simpler equation: There is our equality and those who would prevent us from realizing it. Still, I'm intrigued by the idea of cosmic reckoning, a moral universe in which the meek rise to power, the bad guys get punished, and righteousness rolls down like a mighty stream. The emphasis on a moral universe as opposed to a moral earth is troubling, however. It seems to suggest that justice is to be attained not on this bloodstained ball of confusion but on some other plane of existence, a milk-and-honey realm where lynching victims and rehabbed racists will frolic arm-in-arm. That sounds lovely, if you believe in Paradise.

Out here in these streets, though, moral revolution depends on an assumption of shared values underlying the American experience, what historian Richard Hofstadter called a "kind of mute organic consistency." It depends on a narrative in which majority and minority both want the same things. It depends on a narrative in which oppressors and oppressed are equally culpable. It depends on a narrative in which oppressors earn forgiveness for their centuries-long litany of cruelties through repentance, generosity, and hard work. Repentance on the part of white Americans has been rare and generosity intermittent. In contrast, black forgiveness of their racist transgressions has often been automatic. In many instances of white Americans violently oppressing their black countrymen, the body is *not yet cold* before the dead person's relatives are standing before cameras offering heartfelt platitudes about forgiveness. Do oppressed people have an irresistible impulse to forgive? Does forgiveness free us from some larger burden, enabling us to cope with the daily struggle? Or perhaps it keeps the hot coal of anger from burning our palms, as the Buddha would have it? Loving our oppressors is so much a part of the African American consciousness that to question it is to risk censure of the harshest kind. It's a form of masochism, kissing the sword that has just sliced you open.

Perhaps forgiveness is politically expedient in settings where a numerical minority could otherwise get little done without further bloodshed. But if it makes sense to sometimes forgive as part of a larger political strategy, it does not function so well as a method of advancing moral consciousness in the United States. The Founding Framers had already staked a claim to the nation's moral imagination long before the hunger for captive black bodies reached fever pitch. They polished their Enlightenment-flavored philosophies about morality and the dignity of man while building an economy on our ancestors' backs and making a concerted effort to cripple their spirits and minds. This was, of course, a long, strategic process. In addition to murder, it involved rape, starvation, sleep deprivation, forced labor, mutilation, poisoning of food and water, and denial of access to spiritual materials—techniques most of us will recognize as elements of systematic torture. With hypocrisy, greed, and cruelty woven so tightly into the American fabric, a campaign to improve the country based on an ostensible moral consensus seems Sisyphean indeed. While honorable as a motive, moral suasion is ultimately insufficient as a tactic.

What's more, religion, secular humanism, and atheism have all failed to instill anything like a moral culture in human beings. There is no shortage of cruel, duplicitous, and self-centered people of faith. There is no shortage of cruel, duplicitous, and self-centered secular humanists. There is no shortage of cruel, duplicitous, and self-centered atheists. Can we honestly claim morality exists here in the United States, where inequality has always thrived with the assistance of and on behalf of the state? The worst manifestations of unfair treatment include poverty, hunger, homelessness, substandard schools, untreated illness, and defenselessness against rape and other forms of violence. Half-hearted attempts at Great Societies and wars on poverty have failed to prove that eliminating any of these ailments has ever been a priority of the US government or its citizens for very long. Right-wing attempts to dismantle health care and punish the poor, abetted by the sixty-three million people who voted for a proud advocate of sexual assault, demolish the notion that, as Barack Obama proclaimed in 2008, "we hold common hopes." What we have in common is the fantasy of a social contract. Sustaining the fantasy requires the delusional participation of all of us.

When one takes a slightly longer view of history, the futility of moral campaigns becomes even more evident. Consider, for example, the state of global civilization when Africans first arrived in Jamestown in 1619. At that time, church-led persecution, antireligious violence, human trafficking, child labor, and sexual assault were endemic. Four hundred years later, this still holds true. Human beings haven't developed moral sophistication; we've merely gotten more practiced at developing rationales for our immorality.

> *What, to the American slave, is your 4th of July? I answer; a day that reveals to him, more than all other days in the year, the gross injustice and cruelty to which he is the constant victim. To him, your celebration is a sham; your boasted liberty, an unholy license; your national greatness, swelling vanity; your sounds of rejoicing are empty and heartless; your denunciation of tyrants brass fronted impudence; your shout of liberty and equality, hollow mockery; your prayers and hymns, your sermons and thanks-givings, with all your religious parade and solemnity, are to Him, mere bombast, fraud, deception, impiety, and hypocrisy—a thin veil to*

cover up crimes which would disgrace a nation of savages. —FREDERICK DOUGLASS (1852)

During Obama's first term as president, the audacious hope of his campaign collided with resurgent racism at nearly every level of society. Racism had never measurably decreased; it had merely receded. Bizarrely, Obama's election made it safe to climb out from under the rocks. Before his victory, racism's adoption of soft-power techniques (rebranding, the pseudo-language of conciliation) coincided with a reluctance on the part of progressives to call racism what it is. Many behaviors and policies that were in fact racist (e.g., "welfare reform" and the "war on drugs") weren't labeled as such, ostensibly out of concern for white people's feelings.

Ironically, whenever white misbehavior is actually called out as racist, the denunciations seldom reach their targets. Instead, they arouse spasms of fragility among moderates who consider themselves allies of the black struggle. Any criticism delivered with a hint of passion stirs questions such as "Why are you so angry?" and "What about me? You don't think I'm racist, do you?" A cloud of mutual suspicion forms, hindering insight and prompting fatigue. Black activists return to the streets and strategy sessions while their would-be white supporters retreat to the alluring comforts of silence. For fear of saying the wrong thing, they say nothing at all.

Their reticence clouds the landscape even further, increasing the wariness of citizens working for full equality. A 2006 FBI report notes the activity of "ghost skins," Americans devoted to the delusion of white supremacy who perform their deeds in secret. It enables them to blend into society and infiltrate police departments, political parties, military forces, and other federal and municipal institutions. For African Americans in search of the "true spirit" of this country, knowledge of these covert operations leads to more questions. To what extent do white silence and active-but-illicit racism come between people of color and equality? To what extent do they impede our children's opportunity to embrace the American promise? How can we distinguish between moderates and ghost skins if moderates never express themselves?

If we turn to an earlier period in the struggle for black lives, we find that the timidity of white moderates has always been a problem. Martin Luther King Jr. was a particularly frustrated critic. "I have almost reached the regrettable conclusion that the Negro's great stumbling block in his stride toward freedom is not the White Citizen's Council-er or the Ku Klux Klanner," he said, "but the white moderate who is more devoted to 'order' than to justice; who prefers a negative peace which is the absence of tension to a positive peace which is the presence of justice." In King's view, "lukewarm acceptance is much more bewildering than outright rejection."

While the Lukewarmers shelter in place, outspoken racists, for whom we used to employ the reassuring phrase "lunatic fringe," have entered the telegenic mainstream. Sporting fashionable haircuts, salon tans, and Colgate-totally-whitened smiles, they are devising policy in the executive branch, preaching their racist gospel at universities, and defending police brutality on cable television. Perhaps emboldened by their trickle-down bigotry, their less polished counterparts compete to earn fifteen minutes of YouTube infamy by brazenly terrorizing any African American, Latino, Muslim, Jew, or disabled person they stumble across on a subway train or Walmart parking lot.

This frenzy of grievance affecting numerous affluent, poor, urban, and rural white Americans is symptomatic of the inevitable decline of empire. The browning of our country and falling fertility rates among white citizens stimulate an anxiety of impotence and an outbreak of irrational jealousies. Like Don Cheadle's piano, these neuroses provoke a suspicion that minorities are getting more than they deserve. Acting on those impulses, billionaire policymakers and their elected lackeys conspire to deny basic access to health care, clean water, and ballot boxes. The disruptions unfold in accord with the emergence of well-financed white racist groups on college campuses, and the persistence of Trump rallies packed with his admirers, pounding their chests and hooting.

White moderates undoubtedly know that we are living in an era when, as the *Washington Post* put it, "anti-black sentiments drive white residential preferences." They likely know that 74 percent of white evangelicals, hell-bent for nostalgia, believe American culture has changed for the worse since the 1950s, and that 56 percent, or *more than half* of all whites, agree with them. They've probably seen the NPR poll showing that 55 percent of whites believe they face racial discrimination, as well as the American National Election Study indicating that "black influence animosity" and racial animus were the main deciding factors for Trump voters. They also may have seen the proliferation of Facebook groups for "pissed-off white Americans" and racists whose concept of morality is rooted in a worldview in which black people are little more than pack animals and concubines. When white moderates don't speak out against these troubling developments, is it unreasonable to wonder if they agree with them?

I've noted earlier that "going high" often seems designed

to tiptoe around the sensitivities of sympathetic observers and their fence-straddling cousins. In addition, it creates the unintended consequence of lowering the bar where the support of white "progressives" is concerned. Shouldn't we demand more than lukewarm acceptance from people who consider themselves our allies? In the face of overwhelming racism, is politeness stupid?

They can help raise expectations by going beyond preaching to the converted and actively engaging all those white people who cling to their unearned advantage, stuck in the delusion that sharing opportunity is equal to diminishing whiteness. They need to tell them that people of color don't want what white people have; we want what is rightfully ours. I see and appreciate the allies who march with us, rejoice with us, commiserate with us, and join their voices with ours in a roar of outrage when injustices afflict us. So when I say it's time for allies to do more, I'm not dismissing the significance of their efforts thus far. But they are far from enough.

When they say, "I'm doing all I can," what does that mean? Unless they're challenging the tradition of unearned advantage every day at every opportunity, they are not doing all they can. If they ever indulge in the luxury of remaining silent while people of color feel the effects of racial inequality every day, they are not doing all they can. Some white people are unable to hear people of color when we're not singing onstage or dancing in the end zone; they might see our lips moving, but instead of our voices, they hear a torrent of howling and screeching. We need the voices of our allies to penetrate the din, using their whiteness as a lever and a megaphone. If they are not challenging their racist brothers, sisters, friends, and lovers on a daily basis, they are not doing all they can. Annual discussions over Thanksgiving turkey won't do it; they need to take place on the regular until racism is acknowledged and equal opportunity is real. Frederick Douglass famously offered this advice to young black Americans: "Agitate! Agitate! Agitate!" Certainly he would not object if we extended his wise counsel to white Americans who claim to be committed to equality and justice.

> What gets me about the United States is that it pretends to be honest and therefore has so little room to move toward hope.
>
> —AUDRE LORDE, "TRIP TO RUSSIA"

Along with Douglass and David Walker, Maria W. Stewart was one of the earliest black American philosophers to disseminate her ideas about race, justice, and civic virtue. In 1831, she published *Religion and the Pure Principles of Morality*, a pamphlet that, among other subjects, disputed prevailing theories of black inferiority. "It is not the color of the skin that makes the man," she wrote, "but it is the principles formed within the soul." She also referred specifically to Walker, whose *Appeal to the Coloured Citizens of the World* (1829) endorsed a radical morality in which any man who abetted slaveholders was destined for divine punishment. "Are they not the Lord's enemies? Ought they not to be destroyed? Any person who will save such wretches from destruction, is fighting against the Lord," he wrote, "and will receive his just recompense." According to Walker, black men hoping to get heaven had better commit to fighting "under our Lord and Master Jesus Christ, in the glorious and heavenly cause of freedom and of God." Those who refrained from the struggle "ought to be kept with all of his children or family, in slavery, or in chains, to be butchered by his cruel enemies."

In insisting on their own interpretation of the Bible and in their determination to frame their antislavery arguments within a discussion of good and evil, Walker and Stewart (soon followed by Douglass) helped lay the groundwork for a black liberation theology. Elements of their philosophy helped shape and propel every campaign for black equality that came after, especially the modern civil rights movement in which some (but hardly all) black churches played a pivotal role.

Walker and Stewart were up against the kind of capitalist theology found in an 1837 catechism concocted by Rev. Charles Colcok Jones. He was pastor of First Presbyterian Church in Savannah, Georgia—and owner of three rice plantations where more than one hundred enslaved black people labored. In a passage addressing "Duties of Masters and Servants," he wrote:

Q: What are the Servants to count their Masters worthy of?

A: All honour.

Q: How are they to try to please their Masters?

A: Please them well in all things, not answering again.

Q: Is it right for a Servant when commanded to do anything to be sullen and slow, and answering his Master again?

A: No.

Q: But suppose the Master is hard to please, and threatens and punishes more than he ought, what is the Servant to do?

A: Do his best to please him.

Both philosophers argued that pleasing God had nothing to do with pleasing white people, and that the best way to serve Him was to work for freedom for all. For her part, Stewart expressed little tolerance for patience and moral pleading. In an 1832 speech to the Boston-based Afric-American Female Intelligence Society, she advised, "It is useless for us any longer to sit with our hands folded, reproaching the whites; for that will never elevate us." Walker's *Appeal* mentions love twelve times, but never as an unconditional affection to be freely shared with one's oppressors. "We ask them for nothing but the rights of man," he wrote, "for them to set us free, and treat us like men, and there will be no danger, for we will love and respect them, and protect our country—*but cannot conscientiously do these things until they treat us like men.*"

Douglass never assumed that he and his opponents shared the same moral values, even if they claimed as much. He spoke openly of his contempt for their false pieties. "I therefore hate the corrupt, slaveholding, women-whipping, cradle-plundering, partial, and hypocritical Christianity of this land," he wrote in his famous memoir. "Indeed, I can see no reason, but the most deceitful one, for calling the religion of this land Christianity. I look upon it as the climax of all misnomers, the boldest of all frauds, and the grossest of all libels."

Perhaps, this is a moment for impassioned African American critics to take up the mantle of their predecessors and examine the fraudulent underpinnings of American morality once again. To cast aside "abiding faith" and interrogate the "bombast and fraud" that Douglass identified in 1852. To question America's fundamental pretenses, as Fannie Lou Hamer did in 1964. Without a flourishing and constructive black contrarianism that rigorously engages Manifest Destiny, American exceptionalism, "free" enterprise, and other precious national tenets, we remain, as DuBois said, "the sole oasis of faith and reverence in a dusty desert of dollars and smartness."

In addition, there is no time like our disorderly present for African Americans to have an unprecedented conversation among ourselves about what we think morality is. We need a discussion that isn't predicated on the majority culture's conception, with its historical roots in invasion, abduction, and forced conversion. What's more, the conversation would be incomplete without the contributions of black people whose spiritual practices differ from those of Christians, or who choose to forgo such practices altogether. These discussions would almost certainly be uncomfortable and occasionally contentious, but they are absolutely necessary.

For example, there is nothing close to a consensus about LGBTQ lifestyles. While many of us regard the right to be one's true self as fundamental and unalienable, others among us continue to condemn same-sex-loving and nonbinary peoples as sinners and abominations. Still, others defend outrageous behavior in the name of racial "solidarity" (see R. Kelly, for example). Meanwhile, in some "prosperity" churches, there's no greater sin than insolvency, justice is seldom mentioned, and Jesus is not so much a messiah but a glorified investment broker/Amway salesman who died on the Cross so that his followers could make mad dollars. Do prosperity preachers mean to imply that the poor are impoverished because they're immoral? And while the concept of a hereafter populated by lions and lambs grooving side by side is popular among many religious African Americans, it isn't the only notion of heavenly reward. Historically, even as black people began to accept the possibility of an Americanized here-after, they resisted the suggestion that they would be shar-ing it with their captors.

Charles Ball noted in his 1837 memoir of his life in bondage, "It is impossible to reconcile the mind of the na-tive slave to the idea of living in a state of perfect equality, and boundless affection, with the white people. Heaven will be no heaven to him, if he is not to be avenged of his enemies. I know, from experience, that these are the fun-damental rules of his religious creed, because I learned them in the religious meetings of the slaves themselves."

Is it immoral to adhere to a theology that emphasizes liberation over love, as some of our ancestors did? Is re-fusing to love unwise Supreme Court justices, duplicitous police, and rabid Trump supporters morally indefensible? I'm not against love by any measure, although I want to suggest that it is best reserved for those who love us in re-turn, not for those who oppose us and, in so doing, deny our humanity. How does urging black people to love their oppressors differ from telling a battered wife that her hus-band wouldn't abuse her if he didn't care for her so much? Until we examine such questions thoroughly and with input from a wide cross section of African Americans, we are ill-equipped to launch moral crusades, let alone take them seriously.

We may discover that we have been chasing a unicorn all along. We might realize that as long as there is hunger and other people have knowledge of it, as long as there is wanton killing not only by cops but also by "terrified" pri-vate citizens and self-styled vigilantes, as long as there is predatory lending and for-profit policing, as long as citi-zens remain silent while watching their nominal leaders build fortunes on the backs of the poor and defenseless, as long as there is hoarding of material goods by human beings fully aware that other human beings are dying of lack, there is no such thing as a one-size-fits-all morality. That conclusion is not as pessimistic as it sounds. It would, after all, free us to cast our quest for genuine equality in more earthbound terms. Would it be any less effective, for instance, if we opposed injustice simply because it is unacceptable, not for moral reasons but because *we won't stand for it*?

If we're looking for reasons for optimism, we can find it in knowing that our opponents, despite centuries of concentrated, systematic effort, have failed to completely destroy our minds, our capacity to reason for ourselves. We can find it in our ability to have strong, smart, healthy children despite equally intense efforts to poison, incarcerate, murder, and otherwise inflict them with fatal discouragement. I need no reasons beyond those to motivate my striving. "In the struggle for justice," Douglass observed, "the only reward is to be in the struggle."

I don't believe that love can conquer injustice. Strategy, however, has a fighting chance.

ACKNOWLEDGMENTS

I thank my Ancestors, on whose broad shoulders I stand.

Endless gratitude also:

To my parents, to whom I owe more than I can ever repay. Thank you for life, love, and the inspiration to live thoroughly.

To my many kind colleagues at Emerson College. Your enterprise spurs me to continuous effort.

To my generous former coworkers at *The Crisis* magazine (Lottie Joiner, Wayne Fitzpatrick, India Artis, Reginald Thomas, and Laura Blackburne), as fine a group of journalists as I've ever had the privilege of working with.

To my capable and energetic assistants at Emerson, Jordan Cromwell and JennyMae Kho.

To Joy Harris, for encouraging me to write this book and Adam Reed, for handling tasks big and small.

To Anna deVries, for astute editing and saving me from myself.

To Kolt Beringer, for his adept handling of all the moving parts.

To Josh Karpf, for giving the text a thorough and necessary scrubbing.

To James Meader, Josh Zajdman, and Brianna Scharfenberg for getting the word out.

To my siblings, living and gone, for your wit, warmth, and example.

To my mother-in-law, Susie Ward, for endless kindnesses.

To my five geniuses, Joseph, G'Ra, Indigo, Jelani, and Gyasi. What a life you have given me.

To my wife, Liana. You are far more than moon and stars.

To anyone whom limited space and memory have caused me to omit, please forgive me and know that I am thankful.

SELECTED BIBLIOGRAPHY

GETTING IT TWISTED

Ronald L. Fair, *Hog Butcher* (Evanston: Northwestern University Press, 2014).

Ronald L. Fair, *We Can't Breathe* (New York: Harper & Row, 1972).

Toni Morrison, *Playing in the Dark: Whiteness and the Literary Imagination* (New York: Vintage Books, 1993).

THE ELEMENTS OF STRUT

W. E. B. DuBois, *The Souls of Black Folk* (New York: Penguin, 1996).

Henry Wiencek, *An Imperfect God: George Washington, His Slaves, and the Creation of America* (New York: Farrar, Straus and Giroux, 2004).

SHOOTING NEGROES

Douglas A. Blackmon, *Slavery by Another Name: The Re-Enslavement of Black Americans from the Civil War to World War II* (New York: Anchor, 2009).

Edward P. Jones, *The Known World* (New York: Amistad, 2003).

Solomon Northup, *Twelve Years a Slave* (New York: W.W. Norton, 2017).

COLOR HIM FATHER

Barack Obama, *Dreams from My Father: A Story of Race and Inheritance* (New York: Broadway Books, 2004).

THE SEER AND THE SEEN

Lorraine and Jerrold Beim, *Two Is a Team* (New York: Harcourt, Brace & Co., 1945).

Polly Greenberg, *Oh Lord, I Wish I Was a Buzzard* (New York: Macmillan, 1968).

Polly Greenberg, *Oh Lord, I Wish I Was a Buzzard* (New York: SeaStar, 2002).

Polly Greenberg, *The Devil Has Slippery Shoes* (Washington, DC: Youth Policy Institute, 1990), 74–75, 80, 729, 744–45, 755.

June Jordan, *Who Look at Me* (New York: Thomas Y. Crowell, 1969).

Nancy Larrick, "The All-White World of Children's Books," *Saturday Review*, September 11, 1965, 63–65, 84–85.

Paul McKee, M. Lucile Harrison, et al., *Come Along*, 3rd ed. (Boston: Houghton Mifflin, 1949).

Paul McKee, M. Lucile Harrison, et al., *Jack and Janet*, 3rd ed. (Boston: Houghton Mifflin, 1949).

Dale Edwyna Smith, "The Legacy of Irris Bonner Harris," *Southern Review*, October 1990, 796–80.

Dale Edwyna Smith, *The Slaves of Liberty: Freedom in Amite County, Mississippi, 1820–1868* (New York: Routledge, 1999).

THE THING ITSELF

Chester Himes, *The Quality of Hurt: The Autobiography of Chester Himes*, vol. 1 (Garden City, NY: Doubleday, 1972).

Langston Hughes, *The Big Sea: An Autobiography* (New York: Alfred A. Knopf, 1940).

William Styron, *The Confessions of Nat Turner* (New York: Random House, 1967; 1st Vintage international ed., 1993).

Alice Walker, *You Can't Keep a Good Woman Down* (New York: Harvest, 2004).

Richard Wright, *Black Boy* (New York: HarperCollins, 2005).

Frank Yerby, *The Dahomean* (New York: Dell, 1971).

Frank Yerby, *The Foxes of Harrow* (New York: Dial, 1946).

Frank Yerby, *A Woman Called Fancy* (New York: Dial, 1951).

OF LOVE AND STRUGGLE

Charles Ball, *Slavery in the United States. A Narrative of the Life and Adventures of Charles Ball, A Black Man*, 3rd ed. (Pittsburgh: John T. Shryock, 1853).

Maria W. Stewart, "Religion and the Pure Principles of Morality," Dorothy Schneider and Carl J. Schneider, eds. *Slavery in America: From Colonial Times to the Civil War* (New York: Facts on File, 2000).

David Walker, *Appeal to the Coloured Citizens of the World* (Baltimore: Black Classic Press, 1993).

ABOUT THE AUTHOR

JABARI ASIM was born and raised in St. Louis, Missouri. For eleven years, he was an editor at the *Washington Post*, where he also wrote a syndicated column on politics, popular culture, and social issues, and he served for ten years as the editor in chief of *The Crisis*, the NAACP's flagship journal of politics, culture, and ideas. He is the recipient of a Guggenheim Fellowship in Creative Arts and the author of six books for adults, including *The N Word*, and nine books for children.